WHAT THEY'RE SAYING ABOUT ALEX SWIRE-CLARK

"Interesting, educational, and fun!! 5 Stars!"
  Lynn Bennett, EVP, Coakley & Williams Construction

"Transformative information. Your use of stories and examples was superb."
  Greg Blaisdell, President, Evoke Research and Consulting

"This was very timely for the stage of growth in my company."
  Ken Coleman, CEO, Lewis-Price & Associates

"Captivating examples … of life-altering knowledge."
  Adam Copenhaver, CEO CopenHaver Homes

THE RAPPORT ADVANTAGE

Transforming the Way Leaders Communicate

ALEX SWIRE-CLARK

Palmetto Publishing Group
Charleston, SC

The Rapport Advantage
Copyright © 2019, Alex Swire-Clark

ISBN-13: 978-1-64111-313-7
ISBN-10: 1-64111-313-8

Edited by: Catherine Leek of Green Onion Publishing

To Mom, Dad, Ginger, and the kids. I love you all!

CONTENTS

THE WHEELS ON THE BUS GO OFF THE GROUND

It was the Fall of 1981.

I was in elementary school at the time in a rural southern town.

The school bus I grew up riding was pretty typical. There were all sorts of kids on that bus. There was the kid who as soon as he got on the bus, the rest of the bus called his name, "Hey, Ivan. Come sit here, man!!" He'd take out a pencil, turn it into an imaginary microphone and bust into, "Just a small town girl!!!" Everybody would join in with, "Living in a lonely world!!"

There was the kid who got on the bus and the first thing she did was look for the empty seat so she didn't have to talk to anyone. We had the kid who gave up his seat so that someone else could sit down. We had the kid who was up front, sitting beside the driver asking him/her about how the bus worked, what it was like to drive. We also had the kid who stared out the window.

I would be at the bus stop 45 minutes early so I could get the very first seat. The driver of Bus 43, a high school senior named Sloan, normally passed my road at 6:43 on his way to his first stop before picking up a bus full of kids and then coming back to my road around 7:37 for one of the last stops. I would flag him down, run across the road, get in, and say, "What's up, Slaw!"

Obviously, Sloan wasn't a very common name and I heard everyone else calling him "Slaw" so I just went with it. He'd say, "Hey, Bud" and immediately I would go all the way to the back of the bus and sit down. This was a classic big yellow bus with the classic brown bench seats from front to back, with the characteristic old chewing gum on the floor and ceiling. All of the seats were empty of course.

So I'd sit there and then about 2 minutes into the ride, I'd yell up front, "Hey, Slaw? We gonna go big today?"

"Oh yeah, dude!"

Now you're probably thinking, "Why is Alex yelling to the driver from the back of the bus when there are plenty of empty seats at the front?" Looking back I ask myself that same question. Very illogical. We'll get to that point soon enough.

So the bus fills. My buddy Sam gives up his seat to a girl who wants to sit near one of her friends. Sam calmly gets up to join me at the back. A little later my pal Ivan gets on, high-fiving everyone on the way to the seat in front of me. We're joking around, having a good time. Ivan and I are telling stories. Sam is sitting there listening, laughing along with our jokes. Most of the girls are in the front chatting away except Carla. She's in kind of a dreamy state staring out of the window. Carla usually doesn't have much to say. You could call her shy. Then the bus slows to make a left-hand turn onto Ashe Street.

Now you have to understand that Bus 43 was *the* bus to be on going to school in the mornings because it made a left onto Ashe Street. Halfway down the road there was a hump in the asphalt at the intersection where the road crossed Greene Street. This hump was not very noticeable when traveling over it by car on a normal day … at normal speeds.

As soon as we make the turn onto Ashe Street, people start packing the back of the bus like sardines. Boys next to girls. Friends next to enemies. It didn't matter. David, one of the boys in the front, runs to the back saying, "I'm setting the record today!!" Carla turns and watches curiously. A chant starts to build from the back of the bus. "slaw. Slaw. Slaw! SLAW!!"

Without any hesitation, Sloan floors it! "SLAW SLAW SLAW!!!"

Bus 43 hits the hump at 45 miles per hour (in a 35 mph zone). The back of the bus launches up in the air, and all of us with it. There are screams of terror (AGHHHH!!!) and screams of glee (DUUUUUUUUDDDEE!!!). Kids are flying over the seats, trying to bump their heads on the ceiling. In an instant, the bus lands. All of the now scattered sardines start to get up, shaken not stirred. Ha!

We get to our feet cheering. "That was the best one ever!!!" The chants of "SLAW SLAW SLAW!!!" erupt again. All the while, we can see Sloan's expression in the rearview mirror. He has the biggest grin on his face. We start coasting up the hill toward the school.

David muscles his way back to the front so he can be first off. We pull into the parking lot and start piling out. About two-thirds of us start walking off the bus retelling the story all the way inside the building, high-fiving Sloan on the way off. The other third had either sat in the front and were already off the bus, like David, or stayed on until every-one else got off the bus, like Carla.

Now, if you asked some of those involved to tell you about their experi-ence on the bus that morning, statistics show that there would be four typical, yet distinctly different answers.

1. David, the boy from the front: "I got the most air of anybody. But when it was done, I was ready to get to school and get start-ed." He was clearly focused on getting things done that day.

2. Ivan, the high-five guy: "That was awesome!!!" He's still talk-ing about it 30 years later!

3. Sam, one of the sardines: "Did you see the happy looks on everyone's faces? We had a great time today." Sam was always concerned for the well-being of others.

4. Carla, the curious girl: "I don't think Sloan was obeying the speed limit. I wonder how fast we were going?" Carla was constantly analyzing situations, thinking about the process. She didn't *need* to be at the back of the bus to enjoy the experience.

Four people on the same bus yet, quite different points of view.

As adults, do you think they would approach the purchase of a product or service the same way? Enjoy the same activities? Solve problems similarly? Would they all strive to achieve big hairy audacious goals in their lives?

Of course not. But we think, "Why doesn't my wife like to play on the floor with the kids as much as I do?" Or, "Why is my husband obsessed with making money all the time?"

PEOPLE ARE STRANGE CREATURES

Our minds are wonderfully made. You've probably seen this sample of text on the internet. The brain somehow unscrambles this puzzle and easily reads the passage even though it appears, initially, to be gobbledygook.

> It deson't mttaer in waht oredr the ltteers in a wrod aepapr, the olny iprmoatnt tihng is taht the frist and lsat ltteer are in the rghit pcale. The rset can be a toatl mses and you can sitll raed it wouthit a pobelrm.[1]

How cool is that!

Our brains are extraordinary processors of all kinds of data, capable of reasoning and creativity. Each of us is blessed with a unique way that we view and interact with the world. We all think and feel in totally different ways. We are influenced by our genetics and our environment. It's all quite fascinating.

But people are strange creatures. Why do people do the things they do? It's a question I've been asking myself for years. Why do we do the things we do?

Why do people …

- Put makeup on when they're driving to work? Don't they know that's an accident waiting to happen? You don't need to look like Gal Gadot that very minute do you?

- Buy more at the grocery store than what's on their list? Why can't they just stick to the list? Isn't that why they made a list in the first place?

- Adopt every stray animal that shows up on their doorstep? Isn't three or four or ten cats enough? How about this lady with 1100 cats in her home?[2]

- Get the same thing at a restaurant every time? Where's their sense of exploration?

- Have to be so direct all the time? Can't we slow down a minute and consider what someone is feeling at the time?

- Raise their hand to ask a question at every meeting? Can't the cliff notes version be enough?

- Watch the Hallmark channel? Why are we so anxious to watch a movie that is going to make us cry and then say, "That was so amazing!!!" Seriously? :-) (My wife loves it!)

- Remain silent during a meeting? Why didn't you say anything if you had an issue with what was being presented?

One or two of those scenarios probably apply to you. The majority won't. I can guarantee you that if you had a room of 200 people and asked them to stand up when each of those questions applied to them, you could reasonably predict the number of people who would stand up each time.

The reason is because human behavior is predictable. The questions we, as individuals, ask about other people's behavior are built around our own behaviors. After all, we know ourselves better than anyone else, right? We use our own behaviors as a standard for understanding how others behave.

Unfortunately, when it comes to building relationships, if we use ourselves as the standard for how everyone else behaves, we're going to be in a whole world of trouble. Everyone sees the world differently – just as in my bus story. Yes, that's what all the reminiscing was about. In fact, I can give you an example of how people can observe a situation and come up with four different viewpoints as to what happened, or what they were thinking about during the situation.

David, Ivan, Sam, and Carla all had different experiences because they started with different traits, different temperaments, different personality styles – and these are all predictable if you have the right model.

THE COMMUNICATION SITUATION

Our perspectives are rooted in differing personality styles. This difference affects the way we communicate with others as well. We've all heard the old saying when life hands you lemons, make_____. Yes, lemonade. But that's so 20th century. I would argue, that when life hands you lemons, make Lemon Heads – you know, the little yellow candies. They're bite-sized, they clear TSA checkpoints with no problems, *and* they're easy to throw out to an audience from the stage when I'm speaking!!!

Now in business, and in life, why are we handed lemons? There are all sorts of reasons really.

- **Bad luck.** That guy on the freeway who wasn't paying attention, and then – SMACK!!! He hits you in the side. Now you have to pull over and wait for the police. You're going to be late for work and that all-important presentation you were making this morning. UGH!!!

- **Our own failure to plan.** As of this writing, my oldest daughter is a junior in high school. Junior-senior prom is coming! Have I planned for that? No way. Not financially – those

7

dresses cost a fortune. Certainly not emotionally – my baby's growing up and getting ready to graduate soon. *sniff, sniff*

- **Decisions made beyond our control.** In organizations, you can be vehemently opposed to a new initiative, but as a leader, you are asked to help implement and enforce the requirements of this new policy. Tough stuff kiddo.

> *Personally, I get hit with the, "You're taking the kids to gymnastics tonight, right?"*
>
> *"But the tournament's on and they don't have WIFI!!"*
>
> *"It's just one game. DVR it."*
>
> *Not cool honey. Not cool.*

And then there's plain-old miscommunication. It happens in e-mails. It happens in texts. You know the one where you sent "Hey sweetie. Ready for that romantic dinner tonight?" Except, you sent it to your Mother. And then she answers "Yes!" EW!!!

It certainly happens when we're talking to one another. We say something we don't mean to say. We change the subject without telling the person we're speaking to. We do that multiple pronoun thing.

> *"Sally said Emily was going to meet her at the Mall. But then she decided not to go. So she got angry. Then she sent her this crazy text. Then she took a screenshot and put it on Snapchat." Hold on! Who's mad again? Who posted what? Too many pronouns!!*

Sometimes one word can change the entire meaning of a sentence.

> *My 15-year old daughter and I were in the car on the way home from a voice lesson the other day. We were belting out a karaoke version of "Bring Him Home" from the musical, Les Misérables. We got toward*

the end where the main character, Jean Valjean, is holding a wounded young man, Marius, in his arms. Valjean is trying to get Marius to safety, yet Valjean is older and is struggling himself. It is a powerful and emotionally touching piece, my favorite song in the musical. The climactic portion of the song is near the end when Valjean sings, "If I die, let me die! Let him live!" Now, my daughter isn't quite as familiar with the words as I am and she ends up singing, "If I die, let him die!!!"

Wait, what? Let him die? Sweetie! That's just wrong! I think we need to listen to the soundtrack a little more closely.

But sometimes we say exactly what we want to say the way we want to say it, and it *still* causes a problem.

A friend of mine will ask her husband, "Honey, does this dress make me look fat?" Now, the guy answering that question is in serious trouble. Does he really want to answer that question? There are squirrels and birds outside the window screaming "NOOOOOO!! Don't do it!"

The guy says, "You look nice!" That is a compliment, right? I mean, he didn't say, "You look awful" or "Go change right now you hideous beast from the planet Volax 3!"

But she says, "That's not what I asked."

What's he supposed to say? The real question my friend should have asked was, "Do you think I'm beautiful?" And of course, the answer to that question guys is, "Absolutely sweetheart!"

Sometimes miscommunication is more subtle. What about when:

- You are trying to build rapport or connect with a person and you're just not clicking?

- Two team members can't get along and you can't figure out why?

- You and your significant other are on totally different wavelengths?

- Your sales team can't move people through the funnel and close?

The results of the simplest miscommunication can be life-changing.

- Health-altering stress

- Ruined reputation

- Damaged relationships

What about in the workplace?

- Lost sales

- Increased employee turnover

- Inefficient teams

So what causes miscommunication? We've already established that we can say what we want in the way we want and it can still be taken the wrong way.

Webster's dictionary defines communication as, "A process by which information is exchanged between individuals through a common system of symbols, signs, or behavior." It's a two-way street, the giving *and* receiving of information. Unfortunately, either of those can be the cause of problems.

So here's the key question: What is the mental filter that determines how we give and receive information?

Answer? It's the way we are wired – our temperament and personality. Each person has a unique filter for pushing out information to the world and interpreting incoming information from others. Our individual personality styles are the reason we view and respond differently to the same question or scenario. To put it another way, people are a mystery, but there is a solution.

PEOPLE ARE PERSONALITY PUZZLES

No two people – or pieces of a puzzle – are alike. Yet, each of us put together makes up the big box top that is the world in which we live. People's personalities combine many factors.

- Temperament (the way we're wired)

- Environment

- Vocation

- Education level

- Birth order

- Nationality

- Culture (in the US are you from the South, West Coast, Northeast?)

- IQ

- Family

- Home life (how were they cared for as kids, divorced parents, only child, etc.)

- And, of course, life experiences play a huge role. Someone who had a tough upbringing may look at life differently than someone who was from an affluent family and never had to struggle just to put food on the table.

The Rapport Advantage is going to look at how you are wired, your temperament. That part of your personality is the most predictable.

Because of all the factors listed above, it can be difficult to establish a rapport with people. How do you know what to say and when to say it? What part does body language play? What motivates that person?

From the business perspective, world-renowned sales trainer Brian Tracy has 7 Steps of Successful Selling.[3] Love it. Take a look at the second step in Figure 1.

Figure 1: 7 Steps of Successful Selling

BUILD TRUST AND RAPPORT

I totally agree with Tracy's Step 2.

Webster defines rapport as: "a friendly, harmonious relationship; *especially*: a relationship characterized by agreement, mutual understanding, or empathy that makes communication possible or easy." I want to highlight that last phrase, *"makes communication possible or easy."*

Without rapport, there is no moving forward with Tracy's steps 3 through 7 in the sale process or, really, any worthwhile relationship in our personal lives. Yet, companies spend millions of dollars each year training their people how to close and very little on building rapport. You're never going to get to the close if you don't master the steps that come before it. The only thing that will close is the door when they say no. Remember, "They close the door without rapport."

RA TIP: Without rapport, there is no moving forward with the next steps in the sale process or any worthwhile relationship. We build rapport in a number of different ways but primarily through making observations and asking questions. The key is asking the right questions.

We build rapport in a number of different ways but primarily through making observations and asking questions. The key is asking the right questions. Asking questions based on fundamental psychology.

There is a certain pattern to the way humans behave. Philosophers, doctors, and psychologists have hypothesized about this subject for centuries. We'll touch on these ideas a little later.

Suffice it to say, that when we understand how these personality patterns affect our responses to our environment, we will both speed up the rapport building process, and increase the depths of those relationships as well. That will help you close significantly more sales, build better friendships, create better marriages, etc. You see where I'm going with this?

PERCEPTION PUZZLE

Okay! Let's try another mind puzzle – a little different from the one at the beginning of this chapter.

Grab your pencil or pen (or use your finger on the screen if you're on a tablet or e-reader.) You'll also need a stopwatch/smartphone to time yourself. When I say go, turn to the end of this chapter (page 17) and look at the puzzle. NOT YET!!! I want you to find the number "1" and circle it, then find the number "2" and circle it. You're going to be circling numbers *in consecutive order.* Don't start yet! You'll continue doing so until your timer hits 1 minute.

Set your timer for 1 minute.

Ready. Set. Go!!! (Start your timer!!)

———◆———

STOP!!

How many did you get? The average is between 15 and 22.

Now look at the top of the page between the numbers 82 and 7. Draw a line straight down the middle of the page until you reach the little tick mark between numbers 72 and 89. Now go the left-hand side of the page and find the small tick mark between numbers 70 and 20. Draw a line from there to the tick mark on the other side of the puzzle, between numbers 23 and 9. Your puzzle should now be divided into four quadrants.

Quadrant 1 (Q1) lower right, Quadrant 2 (Q2) upper left, Quadrant 3 (Q3) upper right, and Quadrant 4 (Q4) lower left. You'll notice that the circled number 1 is in Q1 (bottom right). Number 2 is in Q2 (upper left). Number 3 is in Q3. And, you guessed it, the circled number 4 is in Q4. So where's number 5 going to be? Back in Q1, of course. Then 6 will be in _____? Q2. Correct. 7 in Q3. 8 in Q4? You got it? See what we're doing here?

Alrighty, then. We're going to play another game.

When I say go, you're going to look at the same puzzle. This time you're going to place an "X" on the number 1, then an "X" on the number 2, then 3, then 4, and so on. You're going to be placing Xs on numbers in consecutive order starting with the number 1.

Hint: Some of these have already been circled so that should help! :-)

Okay, find page 17 again. Ready with your timer again? Get set. GO!!!

STOP!!

How many did you get? Did you get more the second time than you did the first time? Well of course you did. Why?

You recognized the *pattern!*

The first time you didn't know the pattern, so you experienced a high amount of stress and a low amount of productivity. A minute later – not a day later or a semester in college later – a minute later, after a small set of instructions, you played the same game. But look at the different result!

Figure 2: People Puzzle

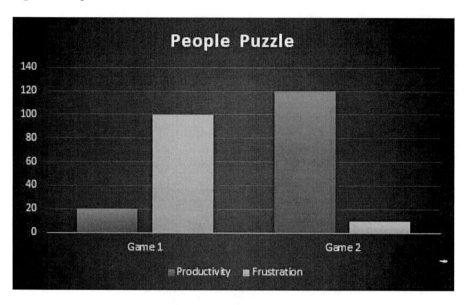

Increased productivity and decreased stress.

There is a way to have less stress and increased productivity in your personal and professional relationships. Even though humans are all unique, there is a *pattern* to human behavior.

Over the course of the next few chapters we're going to outline the DISC Model of Human Behavior to identify these patterns – it will explain so much.

34	94	54	82	7	63	87	43
86	50	10	46	71	19	59	15
58	2	18	90	35	55	27	95
42	26	62	22	79	11	3	67
6	66	30	74	47	83	39	91
70	38	78	14	31	51	75	23
20	84	76	88	49	73	85	9
92	68	4	36	61	17	53	41
44	28	96	12	81	33	21	93
60	16	56	52	69	45	77	5
8	32	40	64	13	29	37	65
80	48	24	72	89	57	1	25

Modified from "Making Sense of Your People Puzzles" by Personality Insights Inc., www.personality-insights.com/shop/making-sense-of-your-people-puzzle-single/

MY PROPOSAL

Why do I use the DISC Model of Human Behavior versus other models like MBTI (Myers-Briggs Type Indicator), the animals, or colors? Let's start with the history of DISC shall we?

THE DISC MODEL

This will be short, I promise. But a little background will set the scene.

We could go all the way back to Hippocrates in 400 BC to talk about the origins of DISC, but let's start with Carl Jung in 1921. The Swiss psychologist and psychoanalyst published *Psychological Types*,[4] where he hypothesized that there were four psychological functions: sensation, intuition, thinking, and feeling.

Move ahead to 1928, when William Moulton Marston published *Emotions of Normal People*.[5] He described the four-personality style theory that is the basis of what we use commonly today. His concepts were adopted by the US military during World War II to more effectively recruit. In the 1950s and 60s, Walter Clarke developed one of the first self-rating assessments, which employed the use of self-describing words and phrases.[6] His appraisal began to be used on a broader scale. Feel free to look up these chaps online to see more details on their research.

DISC language is based on observable behavior. That's why we sometimes mix the terms behavioral style and personality style.

I have found that DISC is a bit simpler to understand and communicate to others. If you understand something and can apply it easily, I feel that you are more likely to put it into practice on a daily basis.

To give you a visual explanation of the model, take a look at the diagram in Figure 3.

Figure 3: The DISC Model of Human Behavior

Did that help? Perhaps a little more explanation is required.

DISCOVER MORE ABOUT YOUR AND OTHERS' PUZZLES

I submit to you that everyone can dynamically transform the way they build rapport and communicate. You can dynamically transform the way you build rapport by following the three goals we're going to cover in this book.

> **Goal #1 – Build the Puzzle's Outline:** Discover the basic personality styles and how they affect the way *you* act and communicate. These are your general tendencies and form the structure or framework of the puzzle.

> **Goal #2 – Fill in the Puzzle's Center:** Expose the more specific personality features and characteristics of each personality style. These are the other pieces in the puzzle box and they fill in the details.

> **Goal #3 – View the Whole Puzzle Picture:** Use the specific tools I will cover to adapt and adjust your personality style to those of others. This will allow you to build better relationships with others, which leads to more sales, more cohesive teams, *and* leads to healthier relationships in your personal life as well. To continue with the metaphor, this is like the top of the puzzle box, giving the big picture.

> **Bonus Goal:** And if you hang in there with me, we'll explore some bonus topics.

> - What is emotional adaptation and why is it so difficult?

> - What is job benchmarking (matching) and how do we use it to increase retention and reduce workplace conflict?

RA TIP: Accomplishing these goals will provide you with a foundation to dynamically transform the way you build rapport and communicate with others in your personal and professional life.

Throughout the course of this book, we're not going to hold hands and sing "Kumbaya" to try to find ways to connect with others. You're going to get practical, tactical knowledge that you can put to work the moment you complete each chapter. Once I have given you the foundational knowledge, we'll dive into some specific applications to put to use right away in your organizations and/or at home.

With this information you'll better speak the language that others use and increase your Rapport Advantage.

GOAL #1
BUILD THE PUZZLE'S OUTLINE

Everyone reacts and responds to the world around them based on their own unique personality style. What do I mean by that? My school bus story is a perfect example – one event, four points of view.

This chapter and the exercises in it will help us facilitate this first goal of finding the border puzzle pieces – the overriding tendencies of our personality styles.

A PERSON'S ACTIVITY LENS

Let's say you're at a party and there's a karaoke machine that gets powered up. Someone pulls up a song, let's say "Staying Alive" by the Bee Gees. The microphone gets put in front of you. How are you going to respond?

If you're reserved, you're going to calmly say, "No thanks" and shake your head. There is no way you are getting up in front of all those people to give Barry Gibb a run for his money. You carefully move away from the attention and find a spot to the side where you can watch the performance.

On the other hand, if you have an outgoing style, you thought they would never ask! Before the intro to the song is over, you've got your jacket off, swinging it around like you own the platform!! "STAYING ALIIIIII IIIIIIIIIIIIIIIIIIIIIIIVEEEEEE!!!!" You soak up the applause like a sponge.

So *outgoing* versus *reserved* are two of the factors we'll discuss in terms of identifying our styles. The point is that two people in the same situation can have totally different reactions to the same circumstance.

The DISC Model asks us two simple questions to help us identify our basic personality style.

1. Are you typically more *outgoing* or more *reserved*?

2. Are you typically more *people oriented* or more *task oriented*?

There is certainly much more to the model and we'll cover that later.

QUESTION 1: ARE YOU TYPICALLY OUTGOING OR RESERVED?

When you are in a large group setting do you want to be in the front singing karaoke or in the back with a small group of close friends? Or, when you are on vacation to recharge are you more likely to look for an opportunity to be with others (party, dancing, games), or would you rather find a quiet place with a hammock and curl up with a good book?

If you answered "being around others" you are most likely outgoing. If you chose the quiet, you're most likely reserved.

This outgoing/reserved question relates to your pace or motor. Everyone's motor is powered differently.

When you stand beside outgoing people, if you listen carefully you can hear their motor sounds – like this, "VROOM, VROOM". You can almost hear their screeching tires as they run off to their next activity or event for the day. They are moving fast. If you listen to a reserved person's motor, it sounds like a nice light hum, "mmmmmmmmmm." They're never going to get a ticket for disturbing the peace!

Outgoing people tend to be:

- Fast paced

- Involved

- Energetic

- Optimistic

- Positive

- Enthusiastic

These are the people with big personalities. Their focus is talking things out.

Reserved people tend to be:

- Slower paced (don't jump into things too quickly)

- Cautious

- Concerned

- Patient

- Steady

- Discerning

These are the people who will think through the various steps to solve a problem, but will be reluctant to share it. They want to look at multiple angles before making decisions. Their focus is thinking things through.

As an outgoing person, I always had difficulty understanding the "motors" of people who are more reserved. My attitude toward them was, "Come on man. Let's go. WOOOOO!!!" They looked at me like, "Dude, what have you been smoking?"

RA TIP: Those of us who are outgoing have to learn to slow down a bit when working or communicating with more reserved styles. Those who are more reserved need to sometimes pick up the pace just a bit. The key point here is that it's not a matter of who's right and who's wrong, or who's good or bad, it's understanding that we're different.

HOW DOES YOUR MOTOR RUN?

We're going to find your pace or motor location on the DISC Model diagram (see Figure 4).

If you consider yourself more outgoing, move your pen to the middle of the top half of the circle and hold it there for a moment. If you consider yourself more reserved, move your pen to the middle of the bottom half of the circle and hold it there for a moment.

If you're intensely outgoing or reserved, then your pen should be near the edge of the circle. On the other hand, if you're not strongly outgoing/reserved, your pen should be closer to the center of the circle but still on that half of the circle. The closer you are to the center of the circle, the more often you have some reserved days and some more outgoing days.

Figure 4: The DISC Model of Human Behavior

For instance, those of us who live on the edge of the circle are much more comfortable being that particular style all the time. I'm very outgoing. There is no question about where my pen goes. I'm an intensely outgoing person. I'm the guy who will talk to a squirrel. My pen goes to the top edge of the circle.

Place an "X" there.

BLENDING DIFFERENT MOTOR TEMPOS

Jim Collins wrote a fabulous book called *Good to Great*.[7] (Crazy to think that it was published back in 2001.) Its core message still rings true. You need to get the right people in the right seats on the bus. For those of you that haven't read it, the bus represents your company, department, church, or other organization. Let's change the bus metaphor slightly by going back to my childhood school bus.

You remember David, Ivan, Sam, and Carla. David wanted to get the highest jump and still be the first one off the bus. Ivan was having fun the whole time. Sam was the helpful, courteous guy. Carla was very analytical about the event that she experienced.

Now imagine if Carla was forced to sit in the back of the bus with Ivan and a bunch of other Ivan-like kids every day. Do you think she would enjoy that? Not a bit. What if David got behind a bunch of slower students as he was trying to get off the bus every day? Don't you think that would drive him bonkers? You bet. If you translate these situations into job roles in your company, organization, or family you can see where conflict might easily arise.

RA TIP: Getting people in the right seats on the bus has everything to do with both skills *and* personality (which includes personal motivators). Ignore using personality information at your own peril!! :-)

To quickly build relationships with others (build rapport), we sometimes have to adapt from where we are to where the other person is. Again, both styles have their great attributes. More on this in the bonus chapter.

If I'm going to a game to watch my North Carolina Tar Heels play, I prefer to go with someone who is more outgoing. I need someone who screams at the officials louder than me! If I'm getting ready to have surgery, I want someone who's more reserved – the last thing I want to hear before the anesthesia kicks in is, "Hey gang. Just for kicks, I'm going to try this one left handed today!" Wait. *What?!?*

Okay, so *outgoing* and *reserved*. Got it? Let's move onto the next principal personality trait to complete the puzzle's border.

> *Alright, Question #2. Here it is!*
>
> *"What is the airspeed velocity of an un-ladened swallow?" OR*
>
> *"Did you order the code red???"*
>
> *"Are you talkin' to me?"*
>
> *"Aren't you a little short for a storm trooper?"*
>
> *"Who's on first?"*
>
> *In case you didn't get any of those, they were famous questions asked from movies 20+ years ago. Can you name the films??*

Okay, seriously … let's move on to question 2 to gain the rapport advantage.

QUESTION 2: ARE YOU TYPICALLY PEOPLE ORIENTED OR TASK ORIENTED?

People oriented folks care about relationships, feelings, friendships. Task oriented people are all about form, function, lists, processes. This people/task question refers to a person's compass.

To ask it in a different way, when you first go to an event with a room full of people, is your first inclination to go toward a group of people (people oriented), or do you find a spot to sit and check your phone to make sure you know what the schedule is for the rest of the day (task oriented)?

Task oriented people focus on:

- Form

- Function

- Programs

- Plans

- Projects

- Process

Task oriented styles like to be direct and correct. Task oriented people take the slogan "Just Do It" to a whole different level. Their focus is on completing to-do lists. They start their day with 32 items on the checklist and they better get every one of them crossed off or there's going to be outrage!

People oriented styles like to share and interact. They love being around others and sharing experiences with them. Group work is highly enjoyable; not so much for the task oriented styles. People oriented folks hate being alone, while task oriented souls often prefer completing projects independently.

People oriented folks focus on:

- Relationships

- Caring

- Sharing

- Emotions

- Feelings

- Friendships

A people oriented individual is all about relationships. His/her focus is on other people and how they feel.

Okay, back to our circles.

WHAT IS YOUR COMPASS SETTING?

Find the "X" you marked earlier. You can flip back to Figure 4 (page 27). I'll wait …

If you consider yourself more task oriented, move your pen directly to the left on your circle and put a dot in the middle of that pie piece, next to the letter you find there. If you consider yourself more people oriented, move your pen directly to the right and put a dot in the middle of that pie piece, next to the letter you find there.

Again, the closer you are to the edge, the more intensely you relate to that characteristic. Closer to the center means you could go either way depending on the day. Everybody with me?

Wherever your dot is, that tells you your most natural style. This is a very rough approximation of your style.

SETTING A COMBINED COMPASS HEADING

These two compass headings (task versus people) appear to be in opposite directions. And, well, they are, but that doesn't mean two people, each with a different setting, cannot work together and build a good relationship. Perhaps an example will help. Great I get to tell another story.

It was the summer of 1997. I had been married not quite 2 years to my lovely wife Ginger. We were nearing the end of the honeymoon phase of our marriage. We began to have an argument here, a little miscommunication there. We hadn't had many arguments of consequence up until that point. This seemingly new trend was not good, and, to be honest, I was concerned.

I came home from work one day and found Ginger crying. I asked her what was wrong. She said, "I'm not sure. It's like we're on two different wavelengths." I agreed.

I told her rather bluntly, "I know, sweetie. To be honest, I feel like you're not meeting my needs, and I'm not sure if I'm meeting yours. I want to fulfill your needs as a husband, but I don't know how." I sat down with her and held her hand. We both were in tears by this point.

I looked at her and said, "We'll figure something out – together."

That was a half empty promise. My intent was sincere. I wanted to fix the issue. The problem was, I didn't know why we weren't on the same page and I didn't know what I needed to do to make things better. I thought to myself, "We are at a marriage crossroads. Fix it forever or potentially start down the road to divorce."

That same summer I had the opportunity to work at the Broyhill Leadership Conference for Teens near Charlotte, North Carolina. I listened to one of the world's experts on personality insights and communication, Dr. Robert Rohm. He said something to me, something that's had me thinking ever since, something that changed what I think about what's important in building effective relationships, understanding people, and avoiding miscommunication – something that saved my marriage.

He said:

> [Ninety]% of all conflict in people's lives comes as a result of not understanding personality differences between those who are task oriented versus those who are people oriented.

Let me give you an example. Let's say you surprise your *task oriented* special someone with a weekend getaway to San Juan.
Here's what her reaction looks like.

- What time are we leaving?

- How long is it going to take to get there?

- Do we have a budget?

- Do we have hotel reservations?

- Do you have a confirmation number?

- What time is the flight?

- What about the kids?

And on and on it goes.

Some of you are sitting there right now thinking, "You must have met my spouse before." The trip and the whole activity become a *task*. It's about getting there, getting the stuff done, and getting back.

> "We *need* to get Mickey Mouse's autograph. It's the only one we're missing."

> "We've *got* to be at the beach at this exact time of the evening to get the picture we want."

That person doesn't stop until those tasks are accomplished.

Now, what happens if you surprise your *people oriented* sweetheart with that same vacation? The reaction might be, "Really? That's so wonderful. We're going to be together. We're going to have a great time! We're going to eat some great food. Can we go snorkeling? Will we see some sea turtles? Where did you say we were going again?" They are all about the experiences and enjoying the time with others.

Now if you don't understand this task/people oriented dynamic, you're going to run into problems. Conflict is coming.

Task oriented folks ask questions like, "Why can't you stay focused?" People oriented folks ask, "Why are you so mad at me?

Task: "Why can't you ask for directions?"

People: "Why can't you be more spontaneous?"

Another situation could be a Father helping his child with her homework. If the Dad is task oriented here's what he thinks, "Let's get this homework done! We've got things to do!" If the child is people oriented she thinks, "I'm just enjoying time with Dad!" She might not understand why Dad is being so pushy. "Can't I have a snack first?" See the pattern here?

Dr. Rohm's words clicked in my brain. I was so excited coming home from the conference that summer. I had a tool that could help my wife and me have a healthy and happy marriage. We took the DISC personality assessments and found out we were total opposites. She's *super* task oriented and I'm as people oriented as you can be. This newfound personality information unlocked the challenges we were having concerning everything from money to what to name our children. I'll share our style blends a little later.

RECOGNIZING AND APPRECIATING DIFFERENT STYLES

Seeing how opposite compass headings can work together to reach a happy place shows us that each component of the DISC Model is important. One motor speed is not better than another, both compass settings will get you to your goal. What is important is to be able to acknowledge the other style and value the differences. Here's another revelation from my youth.

Back in 1982, I had the wonderful opportunity to go to Camp Kanata, in Wake Forest, North Carolina. I had two fantastic camp counselors who I thought were the coolest people ever – Joe and Jeff.

Of course, every cabin had two counselors. In most cabins, one counselor was usually crazy and outgoing. The other was usually a bit quieter and the one you would usually go to when you wanted to have a "what is the meaning of life" type of conversation.

Of course, I wasn't a human behavior expert back in those days. However, looking back, I can tell you that of the two counselors in Cabin 13 in the summer of 1982, I am certain that Joe Preston was an outgoing, people oriented person. He would always make us laugh by telling us funny jokes. Or he would scare us to death with stories of "The Swamp Baby!!" I remember meeting him on the first day. By the end of the day he had the stereo in the cabin cranking out Billy Squire's "The Stroke."

> *"Now everybody! Have you heard? If you're in the game, then stroke's the word!!!"*

Those were good times. Joe and I connected on so many levels. We were both outgoing, people oriented guys. One of my favorite moments as a kid happened after I left camp. Two years later, I was on campus at UNC Chapel Hill for a football game. As we approached Kenan Stadium, I saw this tall lanky dude laughing.

"I know that laugh," I said to myself. "Is that Joe?" I walked a little closer. Yes it was.

"JOE!!!" I screamed.

He turned and without hesitation said, "Alex!" I ran over and gave him a big bear hug. We talked for about 5 minutes, had a few laughs, and then went our separate ways to get to our seats for the game. I never saw him after that. However, thanks to the magic of the internet, I still keep in touch with Joe nearly 35 years later. That's the power of a meaningful connection.

Now my other counselor, Jeff, was a reserved, people oriented person. He and I had calm, thought-provoking discussions. We would talk about family, and what my plans were after camp.

They were both influential on me in different ways.

And that's just it! You can be influential whether you are outgoing or reserved, people or task oriented. You just need to understand who you are – where you're most comfortable, what behaviors are easier for you than other behaviors – and be able to apply your knowledge to those around you.

These concepts work.

As result of applying this information and a ton of hard work, I'm happy to report that my wife and I will be married for 24 years in August 2019.

Now we have a good sense of our key personality tendencies – a good overview or framework. But before we can make the picture crystal clear, we need to know a little more about the style of each quadrant in the DISC Model. The next goal is to fill in the center of the puzzle by talking about what each letter means.

GOAL # 2
FILL IN THE PUZZLE'S CENTER

Knowing if we are inclined to be outgoing or reserved and if we are oriented more toward people or tasks gives us a great framework. To fully appreciate our — and others' — personality puzzles, we must understand each personality style in detail. This is Goal 2!

Make sure you're paying attention to the styles other than yours so you can make powerful connections with these people. If the letter we are discussing is your primary trait (the letter quadrant in which you placed your dot), this will give you insight into how you are perceived. If the letter is not your primary trait, this will give you insight into how those people are wired.

CREATING A PERSONALITY CHART OF YOUR OWN

You have located your dominant quality — the quadrant in which you drew your dot. To uncover your exact blend, you'll need to complete an assessment. They only take about 12-15 minutes to complete.

Shameless plug: Head over to The Rapport Store at: www.personality-service.com/portal/GPPM/store

We have concise assessments for a basic snapshot, versions that specifically look at how you're wired to lead (Leadership Assessment), and even assessments for teens and children. The children's versions come with a bonus. They have a report that you can give to your child's teacher that shows the best ways to get your child to engage and achieve. How cool is that!!

Check out Figure 5 to see what a blank chart will look like.

Figure 5: Blank Personality Chart

Sally Sample				
Personality Style	D	I	S	C
Very High Segment				
High Segment				
Average Segment **(midline)**					← Midline
Low Segment				
Very Low Segment				

You'll notice the chart is divided into five segments – Very High, High, Average, Low, and Very Low segments. The Average segment is also called the "midline" as it falls between the High segment and Low segment on the graph. This is also referred to as the "energy line." One dot will be applied to each column of the chart (D, I, S, C) depending on your level of intensity in the trait. The closer the dot is to the top of each column, the higher that trait is for the person. All dots that are above the average segment are counted into the primary (highest) and secondary (any other above the midline) portion of your unique style blend.

A C/D style blend, for instance, is doubly task oriented, meaning both their primary and secondary traits are on the left-hand (task oriented) side of our original circle graph. This type tends to be hyper focused on getting things done in a logical way.

Whereas, an I/S blend is doubly people oriented. These types are all about relationships. Entertaining and caring for others is what drives them.

Let's look at the various traits and it will become clearer with the list of characteristics and stories that follow. We'll start with the Ds.

THE DOMINANT STYLE

People in the D quadrant like to be in charge. So let them be! When working on projects, allow your Ds to own a piece of it. Make them accountable for people or projects so they feel like they have control.

MAIN QUALITIES

- **Direct:** Fish or cut bait, in or out, they've got places to be. D types can seem short with people. They don't mean to be. They're simply trying to get things done. They are not going to say in six words what they can say in one or two.

- **Demanding:** They're demanding of themselves and others. If they are on a team and someone else is slacking off, not giving 100%, the D will let a superior (and most likely, the slacker) know. If you've ever heard the term "give 110%" you should be able to figure out that a High D invented that term.

- **Decisive:** Ready, Fire, Aim!! Wait a minute … that's not quite right. (Is everybody alright over there?) This style of leading can have unintended consequences as a result. However, Ds are *highly* productive. If I'm in a dangerous situation, I always want a D with me. They are not going to freeze under pressure. They embrace decision-making. They will take action based on the evidence they have.

- **Determined:** If you tell them, "I just don't think you can get that done in time," get ready for a fight!! They are motivated by challenge. They will push themselves harder than anyone else could. They give new meaning to the term "self-starter." We know that when we turn on the navigation on our GPS and plug in our destination we get an expected arrival time. High Ds take this as a personal challenge. "Twenty minutes? No way.

I can get there in fifteen!" Their tires are screeching as they head out of the driveway or parking lot!

- **Doer:** Twelve- to fifteen-hour days are nothing to a D. In fact, they thrive on them. There's usually not enough time in the day to get all the things done on their lists. Entrepreneurs are often this type. They like starting things, seeing success, and then moving on to the next idea or topic. When you hear "serial entrepreneur" think D style.

For each letter, I'm going to give you a *"watch word."* This is a characteristic that you need to be aware of for that trait. I don't mean for it to come across as mean or have you think I'm picking on you. It's simply a trait that appears when that style is under pressure, very anxious, or overly fatigued. The key is being able to recognize this in yourself and others so that we can eliminate the potential negative effects that come with the behavior. I'm going to give a watch word for every style; so if you're not a D, don't get too excited. Your time is coming!

WATCH WORD: DEFIANT

Sometimes Ds do whatever it takes to get the job done. There might be a little collateral damage, but that's just the way it is. Remember the GPS example we used a minute ago. Ds can sometimes think that the ends justify the means in how they approach things. Ds need to be careful to stay within the rules given to them for a project or assignment. If you want to try to bend those rules, ask first.

LIVING WITH A HIGH D SPOUSE

We took a "family trip" to Disney World in November of 2016. Notice I didn't say vacation. If you have young kids, or had young kids, you know that any type of trip away from home with young ones is anything but a vacation. Constant counting of children. Constant bathroom stops.

To compound that, take that trip with a High D spouse. Check out my wife's Personality Chart in Figure 6.

Figure 6: Ginger's Personality Chart

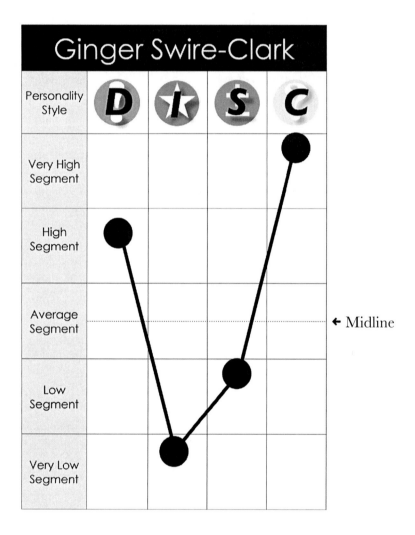

Ginger is a C/D style blend. Both her C and D traits are above the average segment. As mentioned earlier, a C/D style blend is doubly task oriented.

RA TIP: The left side of the graph (Cs and Ds) are typically intrinsically motivated, the right side of the graph (Is and Ss) are typically extrinsically motivated.

C/D blends have little empathy and even less patience. Before we ever booked our first ticket, she had the trip planned out to the minute. We were going to get to *all* the rides and see *all* the stops on the list before we were done.

The first 2 days were Disney Studios and Magic Kingdom. We had a blast. We saw Elsa and Anna from *Frozen*. We sang along as snow fell on our heads. We toured the Magic Kingdom and rode Space Mountain several times. On both days, we were there before the parks opened and we left when the parks closed. Fast forward to day 3.

We arrived at Disney's Animal Kingdom at 8:00 in the morning. We power walked (more like roller derby with a stroller) our way to the Safari ride as fast as we could go. We waited over an hour to get on. Once we got on the ride, it was fantastic. The safari trucks were full but the kids got great seats. While on the ride, we had to wait 10 minutes in the middle of the road for a giraffe to move across our path far enough so that all the safari trucks could proceed with the tour. We got so close to the giraffe that its tail whacked our son in the face! At any rate, we finished that ride, walked through Africa (lions, zebras, and other fascinating animals) and then to the Everest roller coaster. It's about 11 o'clock by now. Our 9-year-old, Jillian, says, "I'm hungry."

Six-year-old Thea chimes in, "I'm tired. Can we take a break?"

Clearly, whining was not on my wife's schedule. Ginger said, "Sure. But don't you want to see the Nemo show?"

Thea said, "I want to go back to the hotel and play at the waterpark."

"Yeah, me too!! The waterslide there was awesome."

My wife didn't understand. "But we haven't even finished seeing half of the park yet." She pulled out the list of what she had planned for us. She held it up. It was long. "We've got Asia, Rafiki, Nemo, the Lion King, and pictures with Mickey and Goofy."

Our 11-year-old son, Jude, pops in, "Mommy, there's no way we're going to get to all that!!"

My wife's expression instantly changed. If you're old enough to remember Bill Bixby in *The Incredible Hulk* TV show, you know the transformation that happened next. My wife went full Bruce Banner gamma rays. RAHHH!!!!!

She said, "You don't think so?"

I just looked at our children, shook my head … and took a couple of ibuprofen.

Needless to say, we saw *everything* on the list. We got back to the car at around 8:00 that night. The kids were tired, grumpy, and ready to go to bed. Until they got back to the hotel and saw the lights on at the hotel waterpark. They were rewarded for their perseverance with some waterslide time. Oddly enough, the kids still talk about the fun they had going to see Nemo and my son winning two stuffed animals at one of the park's game stations after all the complaining started.

Moral to the story? Don't mess with Mom. And more precisely, don't issue a challenge to a High D Mom.

BASIC NOTES

- They make up 10% of the population. They are the smallest percentage of all the personality types.

- Examples: Judge Judy, Mark Cuban, Simon Cowell.

- Ds like challenges, choices, and control.

RA TIP: Perhaps it isn't surprising that Ds make up only 10% of the population. They tend to be high achievers and we can't all be leaders. A High S can make a great complementary style for a High D due to the wonderful supporting nature of a High S. They bring a compassionate perspective that High Ds sometimes need.

THE INSPIRING STYLE

Dr. Martin Luther King, Jr., was a great inspiration to the nation. His charisma was evident. Approximately 250,000 people traveled to Washington, D.C., to hear his "I Have a Dream" speech not knowing that it was going to be one of the most famous speeches ever delivered.

MAIN QUALITIES

- **Influencing:** A lot of High Is gravitate toward … SALES!!! (Imagine that?) They want to convince others of their point of view. They want to mold people. Think about that crazy teacher who tried to make all the students laugh. Chances are he/she was a High I.

- **Impressionable:** The last movie they saw/thing they ate/ trip they went on was the best movie they've ever seen/thing they've eaten/trip they've been on. Two days ago is an ancient memory to most High Is.

- **Interactive:** The worst punishment for a High I teenager? Take their phone away. After 10 minutes they're already in withdrawal. *(Can't … function … Must … check … (insert current social media app here).)* High Is are known to be fidgety. They can't sit in a meeting without something else to do like tap a pencil, check their phone, or doodle. They've always got to be doing *something.*

- **Impressive:** Big body language. Lots of laughs. They are usually the ones telling the jokes at parties, trying crazy things to get a laugh, or being the first to hit the karaoke machine. When you see that YouTube video of a kid trying something crazy, it's probably an I. They certainly coined the expression, "Hey everyone, watch this!"

- **Involved:** Typically involved in many activities to small degrees, versus very involved in one activity. These are the kids on the prom committee, Honor Society, volleyball team, Spanish club, and concert band. As long as there are lots of fun people involved, High Is will show up.

Is, we love you. But sometimes you can be a bit …

WATCH WORD: ILLOGICAL

Oftentimes there's no method to the madness. Because you are not task oriented, you can be a bit disorganized or forgetful. I should know. I'm one of you. And I can prove it – look at my graph in Figure 7.

My wife can send me to the grocery store with a list of ten items and I can come back with nine quite easily. Seriously, Alex? Yes. Let me explain.

Celery will be on the list. I'll walk into the grocery store and head over to the produce section first. I see the celery. I push the cart in front of the celery display. I lean over to choose a bag when I hear, "Hey, Alex!"

"Paul! What's up man?" (My cart now steers itself closer to Paul so I can more easily talk with him.)

"Nothing much. Same ole same ole. When are we playing tennis again?"

"I don't know. It's been a while. How about next week?"

"Sounds good. I'll check my calendar and shoot you a text."

"Awesome! Be good!"

Figure 7: Alex's Personality Chart

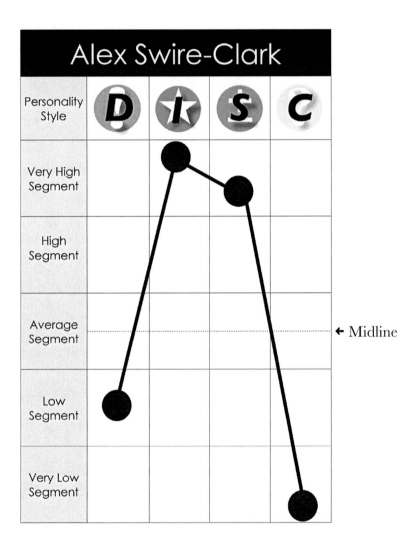

Paul walks away. I continue with the next item on the list which is bread that happens to be very near where Paul was standing. I grab the rest of the items on the list, pay, then head back home.

When I get home my very detail-oriented wife asks, "Where's the celery?"

"What do you mean, 'Where's the celery?' I got everything on the list."

"There's no celery in the bags."

"Well, of course, there … Uh oh." I totally forgot to go back over and grab the celery after I walked out of the produce section. Now I was *in* the produce section. I had *looked* at the celery. I even leaned over to *pick up* the celery. But then, shiny object syndrome (SOS) took over and I neglected to get the celery.

"Nine out of ten isn't bad, right?" I said with a hopeful smile. My smile was met with a look of frustration, but understanding. I smiled back and then turned right back around to make the 5-minute drive back to the store. The famous Gran's Dip recipe required celery. So I went back out to get the celery.

RA TIP: The understanding look in my grocery shopping story is key. Without that Ginger would continue to get frustrated with me every time I came home without 100% of the items. My wife and I are both aware that I can get distracted sometimes. So now when I come home from a normal grocery trip, we agree that 90% of the list is a *win*!

All you non-I types. Cut us a little bit of slack. We're trying hard, but SOS happens – #thestruggleisreal.

One of the best things you can do for an I is to publicly praise them. In front of the organization/class/group, tell them, "You did such a great job, we're going to give you a gold star!!!"

The I says, "Yeah!" They raise their star in triumph and wave their hands to the crowd like they're a rock star. Now let's look at the D style response to that same situation.

"Hey, High D, you did such a great job, we're going to give you a gold star!!!"

The D simply looks you dead in the face and says, "You can keep your star. Who needs that?" Ds react that way because they are intrinsically motivated. Is need a bit more recognition.

THE IS HAVE IT, OR MAYBE WE DON'T

We Is can certainly do some illogical/wacky things sometimes. Here's a case in point.

Back in the summer of 2007, I wanted to get into the sport of paintball. It's a good form of exercise, an adrenaline rush, and I'm used to shooting things having grown up target and trap shooting. I saved up some money. I did my internet research to determine which marker to buy.[8] I decided what gear to get. Now I just needed to find a place to play.

The closest field that had someone who would communicate with me was an hour away in the foothills of the Appalachian Mountains. One Saturday morning, I grabbed my gear, hopped in the car, and headed to Walhalla, South Carolina. I parked at the field and put all my gear on. I went into the pro-shop and spoke to the owner. I gave him a high five and said, "I'm ready to play some paintball!"

He looked at me straight-faced and said, "You've never played before have you?"

"No sir! But I'm excited to be here," I said with a smile.

He looked out of the pro-shop door and yelled, "Hey, Randy. We've got a newbie here!" He pointed me in the direction of a heavy-set fellow who had some pretty cool-looking gear.

I walked over to him, introduced myself, and he began to explain some of the rules of paintball. After about 10 minutes of chit chat, it was time to hit the field. As we're walking onto the field, he said, "So you've never played before, right?"

"No, sir, I haven't."

"So you've never been shot before, then?"

"No, I haven't. I've been wondering ..."

WHACK!!

He shot me in the foot from 5 feet away. Paintballs are shot at a velocity of around 280 feet per second – 280 feet. That's basically the length of a football field. I was shot from less than 2 yards away. I started hopping up and down in pain like a kangaroo on steroids. "Why did you do that?"

He said, "If you can take that, you can take a hit from anywhere else on the field." He was right. I never had a worse hit.

I got out on the field for that first game and I wasn't worried about getting hit because I'd already been shot as bad as it was going to get. I came home with a bruise on my foot but confidence in my head. From there, I ended up joining a scenario paintball team, Team Capital Offense, where I would be named team captain in late 2016.

Fast forward to 2017 and our 11-year-old son decides he wants to play his first game. He invites his best friend, our next door neighbor's son, to go with us.

I told them both, "Before we go, you need to get shot so we all know you can take it."

They said, "Sure thing!" They both went and grabbed their safety gear. They put it on and joined me in the backyard. I sent them over 50 yards away across the yard, facing away from me.

I yelled toward them, "Now don't move, this isn't going to hurt ... much!" I sent a few balls over their shoulders. They could hear the paint whizzing by. I decided that I would aim for the back of their legs just to be extra safe.

I sent a ball down range that rose a bit. It hit my son's friend right in the back of the head. He immediately jumped in the air and then walked away to his left with his thumb up. I quickly put one into my son's back. He dropped to the ground like a lump of coal. He gave me the thumbs up too. After about 15 seconds, he started to get up and I shot him in the back of the leg.

"Hey, what was that for?" he asked as he rolled on the ground again.

"I've got to be harder on you. You're my son!"

"You don't *have* to be!"

I laughed. He wasn't laughing though. I am happy to report that both young men were perfectly fine. After all, if it was dangerous, they wouldn't let you play. They both still tell their "war stories" about getting shot by "Jude's Dad." They had a great time that weekend on their first paintball outing. Neither was scared to be hit.

Moral to the story? Is can be illogical. Shooting paintballs at your son just for fun doesn't make a lot of sense. But we all ended up having a good time shooting at the opposing team later that weekend.

BASIC NOTES

- 25-30% of the population. We definitely need laughs from these folks.

- Examples: Robin Williams, Oprah, Elmo.

- Is like recognition and awards.

RA TIP: Is are great creative, outside-the-box thinkers. What they lack in organizational skills they make up for with wonderful ideas.

THE SUPPORTIVE STYLE

Supportive personality styles make great vice presidents but don't want the limelight. As you saw on my graph I am a High S as well. I am an I/S style blend. If you're an S reading this, how many of you have ever filled out the Panera or Olive Garden survey on the receipt after someone did a great job? Me too!! We like helping others. Along those same lines, an S will be a loyal supporter of a leader through good times and bad if they are treated well and are appreciated.

MAIN QUALITIES

- **Steady:** Ss are the glue of every organization. Steadiness is such a wonderful trait. Unlike the Is, who live on a roller-coaster, the Ss never get too high or too low. They simply keep doing what they do. I hire as many Ss as possible for the "non-drama" factor.

- **Sincere:** They care deeply. Kindness is one of most wonderful traits that we as humans possess. Sadly, it is also one of the most underappreciated traits. To paraphrase Professor Albus Dumbledore of Harry Potter fame, "Just like your Mother, you're unfailingly kind. A trait people never fail to undervalue, I'm afraid." Don't let that stop you from being kind to others. It's the golden rule after all.

- **Sentimental:** I'm about as sentimental as it gets. I was the junior high kid who was the shortest kid in school – read: zero girlfriends. *(All together now … Awwww!)* That was pretty depressing. I used to wallow in that misery by listening to cheesy 80s love songs before I went to bed. (See my fondness for 80s love songs in my LinkedIn Profile – *"I wanna know what love is; I want you to show me!"*) Now, as an adult I've gotten taller. No more of that sappy stuff for me. Okay, fine. I cried during the Disney movie *Tangled*.

What? You cried during Tangled? *Where do you even cry in that movie? None of the good characters die. (Spoiler Alert!) Everyone lives happily ever after.*

Let's think back to that scene where Rapunzel and Flynn are on the boat watching the lights, the result of the bargain she struck with Flynn. This is all Rapunzel has ever wanted. She's staring up at the beautiful lights. Then a beautiful duet begins.

"And at last I see the light. And it's like the fog is lifted. And at last I see the light. And it's like the sky is new."

My 15-year-old daughter is sitting beside me in the theater. She leans over and puts her head on my shoulder and takes my hand.

The song continues, "All at once, everything is different; now that I see you."

At this point she's crying. I'm crying. My little girl is almost grown up. She's going to meet someone and fall in love. Then she won't be Daddy's girl any more. I lean over and give her a kiss on the head and whisper to her, "I love you, sweetie." It was a powerful moment, one I'll never forget.

As I walk out of the theater, I give the usher my "Man Card" as I'm never getting that back! I can say for certain, it was worth it. Because I wasn't afraid to share my emotions with her, it strengthened our relationship, and made a wonderful memory for both of us.

- **Status Quo:** They don't like to rock the boat. They don't like change. If you look on my desk, you'll see one kind of pen: Pilot G-2 0.5. It's all I use. If someone comes into my office and replaces my pens with some other brand, I would probably freak out! The same thing applies with clothing. I've got a closet that has several different styles but, I wear the same eight to ten shirts all of the time. There's a sense of comfortability in that. Status quo also means that they don't like taking risks. They choose investments that are very conservative. They will seek out choices that sacrifice growth for safety. This is why Ss in leadership roles are more conservative in their growth strategies than their High D counterparts.

- **Shy:** Now because my I is so high, I don't have this trait stand out in my I/S blend. I do know many High Ss who are quite shy. Trying to get them to give their opinion is like trying to get a stop sign to turn blue. Good luck! Ss avoid conflict like the plague. They would rather sacrifice their own happiness to eliminate arguments. This leads to deference in other areas. Ss don't usually like to be decision-makers. When my High D wife asks what we should do for dinner, it leads to a frustrating circle for her based on my typical High S response.

My Wife: What should we do for dinner?

Me: I don't care. What would you like? (High S being supportive) :-)

My Wife: Why do I have to choose every time?

Me: You know I don't have an opinion one way or the other. How about Italian? (High S being supportive) :-)

My Wife: No. We had that last week.

Me: Okay, how about the new seafood place?"

My Wife: No, I heard their shrimp wasn't great.

I will keep offering places that I know she will like because I want her to enjoy dinner. Again, I don't really have a preference one way or another. It goes back to one of those basic fundamentals that the male population learns when they are married. In fact, I think Moses probably thought about writing this down as a potential 11th commandment: "Happy wife, happy life!" Can I get an Amen out there?

WATCH WORD: SUCKER

The hardest word in the English language for High Ss is "No." They can be easily influenced if they're not careful. When a timeshare salesperson sees a High S, they start to lick their chops.

Ss want to see the good in others. They are glass half full people. Sometimes this allows them to be taken advantage of.

THE QUIET PASSION OF AN S

Don't mistake all those main qualities for a lack of zeal, but they often express it in an understated manner – because they are reserved. Here's another story to demonstrate.

I'm 17 years old and driving back from my friend Mike's house in my 1984 Pontiac Fiero (tiny, two-seater sports car/fire trap). It's mid-afternoon. The 80s rock hits are playing. I'm coming down Leak Avenue that has these huge oak trees on either side. I'm passing my cousin Mac's house when a squirrel jumps out into the road.

NOOOOOO!!! I hit the brakes, locking my hands onto the steering wheel. SCRREEEECCHH! BUMP. Oh no!!! I ran over the poor little squirrel.

I put my hazard lights on in the middle of the road and quickly got out. He was very still on the warm black asphalt. Being the High S that I am, I did the only thing I knew to do. I was going to do what I could to save "Sammy" the squirrel (assuming he wasn't dead already).

I knew I shouldn't pick him up because according to my Mom, squirrels carried rabies, malaria, and the plague, so I channeled my inner boy scout. I retrieved my car windshield sun visor. I proceeded to try to scoop the little guy off the pavement. This was not easy to do as the sun shade was obviously meant for different purposes. Somehow I managed to get him on the edge of the sun shade and gently slide him down to the middle so that he was ready for transport. I rolled him up in sun shade like he was a squirrel burrito to make sure he didn't fall. I opened the passenger's door and set him and the shade down on the floor board. I turned off the flashers, then did a quick three-point turn and headed straight to the vet clinic where my good golfing buddy, Dr. Forbes, worked.

About two-thirds of the way there I heard a rustling from the floor. I took a glance down and noticed the little guy had his eyes open. Of course, as soon as I saw that I went into full Batman Dark Knight mode. "Hang in there!! Don't you give up on me Sammy!!" I turned the flashers back on. Sammy's critical condition gave me, the teenager, an excuse to speed. I dropped it into third gear and took off.

By the time I arrived at the animal clinic, Sammy was fully alert. I hopped out of the car and ran inside to tell Doc Forbes what had happened. He was finishing up a surgery and told me he'd be right out. He looked at his assistant John, and said, "John, grab your gloves and bring him on in." I turned to see who Dr. Forbes was talking to. John was a mountain of a man. Think Michael Clarke Dunn's character, John Coffey, from *The Green Mile*.

John came outside with me to the car and took a peek inside the passenger window. Sammy had managed to get himself off his back and was now on his side. John put on his gloves while walking around to the other side of the car and said to me in a low voice, "Wait right there." He opened the driver's door and slowly slid himself into the driver's seat. He closed the door with a thud. Big John was squeezed pretty tightly into my little Pontiac.

Sammy sat straight up. John and I were both surprised by this. John reached over to gently pick up Sammy from the floor. Suddenly, the squirrel leaped into the air and onto the passenger's seat. From there, he leaped onto John.

What happened next was a whirlwind as John's face turned from compassion to fear as Sammy jumped on his arm and then back to the seat and then back onto John's head. "Come here you!" John screamed. My little car was rocking back and forth as John grabbed and missed. Sammy was bouncing around the inside of the car like the shiny metal sphere in a pinball machine.

After what seemed like 5 minutes of this, John finally was able to corral the little guy. Sammy fought and bit John's gloves trying to get away but it was no good. John brought him into the doctor who gave him a quick look. Sammy barked the whole time. RAGHH RAGHH!!!

Doc looked at me and said, "He looks good to me. We'll give him a shot of penicillin just in case."

Sammy didn't like that needle going into his backside very much.
I asked, "So what do we do now?"

Doc said, "We let him go."

"You mean right outside?"

"Sure! He'll be fine."

We opened the back door of the clinic. John carefully put Sammy down. Sammy jumped out of John's hand and scampered across the yard to a nearby tree. Up he went. I smiled.

Doc said, "You sure went through a lot of trouble for one little squirrel."

I said, "I wasn't going to let Sammy die because of me."

Ss have what I call "quiet passion." They don't jump up and down and let you know about the things that mean a great deal to them. However, when it comes to things they are passionate about, try standing in their way. You won't be standing long.

BASIC NOTES

- 30-35% of the population. They represent the largest percentage of all the types.

- Examples: Aunt Bee, Mother Theresa, Abraham Lincoln.

- Ss like appreciation and security.

RA TIP: Children who are Ss are some the most easily influenced by peer pressure. Remembering that all peer pressure isn't bad, use this information to help them find peer groups that support the values and ideals that you believe in.

THE CAUTIOUS STYLE

The "measure twice and cut once" saying most certainly came from a High C. And whatever you do, don't let a High I get hold of the project unless you want it destroyed! High Cs are slow to jump into projects before they have all the answers. Here's a great example.

Our family purchased a new home back in 2013. We chose the paint color that the builder provided. Neither of us liked it as much as we thought we would. When we had saved up some money, we decided to put another color on the walls.

My wife, the High C, had to make sure the color was *exactly* right. So what did we do? We bought samples of 15 different shades of brown/gray/beige sample paint to put on the wall. (Thank goodness they were on sale that weekend.) Over the course of that weekend our downstairs family room wall became this striped brownish grey zebra-looking display of color. We had them all side by side to compare. It should have been easy to pick one of the 15 colors, right? Wrong.

The light in that room changed during different parts of the day. She liked one shade from 9 a.m. to 1 p.m. and then a different shade from 1 p.m. to 6 p.m. So what did that lead to? Analysis paralysis. Neither of the two shades was perfect. UGH!! Those colors sat on the walls for months.

We finally had an interior designer friend come in and say, "Do you trust me?"

"Sure we do."

"Get Useful Gray. It looks good everywhere, all the time."

That's what we got and my wife loves it. I got to remove the zebra stripes that had been up for months. She had a third party professional provide assurance of what would look good.

Cs sometimes struggle when committing to projects and committing to relationships because they seek perfection.

MAIN QUALITIES

- **Conscientious:** They're on time. If a C says they'll be there at 9:00, they'll be there at 8:30, ready to start at 8:45, so at 9:00 they don't waste a minute. If an I says they'll be there at 9:00, do you know what that means? Nothing! They might still be at Starbucks talking with their friends about a video they just saw.

- **Competent:** Intelligence is one of their strengths. When you think of competent, think of surgeons, engineers, accountants. These folks love facts and data because there is a beginning and an end. That makes sense to them. It's freeing for them because it's based in logic.

- **Contemplative:** Cs are huge thinkers. They focus on process and are very internal in terms of how they recharge and deal with stress.

- **Correct:** Cs are quite often the smartest people in the room. As young children, this can be problematic for them as they will not hesitate to correct anyone, adults included, if they believe that the person is wrong.

   "Ms. Smith, the answer to the problem is 48 instead of 45."

   "I'm sorry?"

   "You did it wrong."

The adult takes the corrective comment as disrespect when the child is simply trying to eliminate an error. Now granted, there needs to be some polish on the way they share the fact that the problem is indeed incorrect. Boys and girls out there, tact is your friend! :-)

To give you an example of how right Cs are, let me tell you how each personality style apologizes.

- Ds: "SORRY!!!" They say it loudly with a frown on their faces.

  » Wait, was that an apology? Did I do something wrong? Why are they yelling?

- Is: (Laughing) "Sorry! Are we good now?"

  » They want to get back to having fun as soon as possible.

- Ss: "I'm so sorry I hurt your feelings. How can I fix it?"

  » Ss are the style that shows the most kindness.

- Cs: .... They don't apologize! (They're never wrong!)

- **Consistent:** They enjoy doing things/eating things/organizing things the same way based on logic. If they have been to a restaurant before, Cs know what they want on the menu the moment they pull up to a drive-through. This is what it sounds like when my wife, again an off-the-charts High C, drives up to the Taco Bell drive-through with me, the off-the-charts I, in the passenger's seat.

  "Welcome to Taco Bell. Can I take your order?"

High C Wife: Yes, two chicken soft tacos and a medium Pepsi please.

Attendant: Will that complete your order?

Wife: No … (She says this with a look of frustration and then slowly looks over at me.)

The High I's turn: Um, let me see. (It's like I've never been to Taco Bell in my life.)

Me: Yes. … What comes on the crispy chalupa?

Attendant: It comes with WAWAWA. (Insert Charlie Brown teacher voice here.)

Me: Okay, great. Do you have any specials going on today?

Attendant: Yes, we have the WAWAWAWA.

Me: Okay, I don't think that I will be interested in that to-day. (My wife's eyes begin to shoot laser beams at me.)

Me: Fine, okay. One taco please.

Attendant: Okay, will that be hard shell or soft? (My wife just shakes her head. AAAAGHHHHHHHH!!!!!!)

Cs don't understand how a High I can*not* know what they want at a restaurant. They have seen the menu hundreds of times and yet they don't have their mind up as they pull up to order.

WATCH WORD: COLD

Take some time to smile more. Don't be afraid to be a teeny bit sponta-neous. It won't hurt you!

FROM CAUTIOUS TO CONTEMPLATIVE IN A FLASH

Here's one of my favorite stories – because it involves my daughter and my wife.

It's 2002 and my wife Ginger and I anxiously awaited the birth of our first child. Like so many other couples, it wasn't the simplest of processes to get pregnant. Once we did find out we were expecting, we followed the traditional path for American couples. A stereotypical thing that new expectant couples do is a child birthing class. Now, I wasn't incred-ibly excited to participate in these classes, but I'm a High S. So if this would help my wife then I was ready to roll!

So we got to our first class. There were about ten other couples there, each in various stages of the pregnancy timeline. The instructor started with a nice little 5-minute talk about the wonder of parenthood, how our lives will never be the same, how no one can truly prepare you for it. I was thinking, "That's so nice."

My wife was thinking, "Talk to us about breathing. What the husband's role should be? What can I expect to happen at stage 2?"

I was taking this all in. After all I'm a strong S. I want to be supportive. But, I'm an even Higher I. So when we were working on breathing exer-cises, I had to keep it fun. "You can do it, you can do it, go sweetie go!"

My wife, a fervent High C, wanted to have a plan. She had every detail down about the bag being packed, what bottles we would use, breast-feeding or not, etc. After several classes and conversations, we decided to initially try natural childbirth. However, if the pain became overwhelming, she would get an epidural. That was the plan. Got it!

It was a late November morning. I was woken up by my wife at 5:23 a.m.

"I'm having contractions. I think it's time." My brain went into high alert. *("Attention all personnel. Go to DEFCON three. Repeat, we're now at DEFCON three!!")*

We grabbed the hospital bag, which was already by the front door. We hustled to the hospital. Check in was a snap as Ginger had us already pre-approved for a bed. They were waiting for us. After about 30 minutes, the doctor came in and said, "You're having a baby today!" They broke her water a few minutes later and then the real labor began.

For you husbands out there who have experienced this process, you know it can be maddening. Seeing your wife in pain with very little you can do about it is a bit traumatic. After a couple of hours of pain, with no drugs or epidural, she got on a birthing ball. The nurse and I began working with her to help her get through the contractions. I was being as supportive as I could be. After about 45 minutes I began to see the pain on her face. Alex to the rescue!!

"Okay, honey. Let's breathe! Just like we did in class. In 2, 3, 4. Out 2, 3, 4."

My wife looked up at me, her face slightly red and in noticeable pain. She grabbed me by the collar and screamed, "I'M NOT BREATHING WITH YOU!!!!"

Somehow, the nurse overheard my wife's subtle words and gently pulled me to the side. The nurse said calmly, "Honey, why don't you go get some ice chips."

I sprinted down the hall with my Styrofoam cup to the ice machine, filled it up, and ran back. I spent the next hour and a half in the opposite corner of the room holding a spoon and a Styrofoam cup full of ice, just waiting for the nurse to give me my cue.

She said supportively, "Ginger, you're doing great. Let's get you something cool. Ice chips please!" I ran across the room, gave her some ice chips, smiled, gave her the thumbs up and then quickly made my way back to my post.

Then something interesting happened. Ginger stopped talking to the nurse, and everyone else that came into the room. She closed her eyes and just started taking deep slow breaths. This went on for several minutes where she seemed oblivious to me and everyone else in the room. She ignored the rest of the world and put her focus inward to manage the intense pain she was feeling.

Now I tell that story to say this.

My wife is an off-the-chart C. She is *mega* task oriented. I was trying to help her in the way we had both agreed to. After all, she was the one who wanted to go to the maternity classes. She was the one who wanted a plan. But in that moment of pain and anxiety, she returned to her true self. She got contemplative. *She* could do this herself. She focused her energy internally to make it through.

> **RA TIP:** Many times the best way to help High Cs is to simply be there for them but let them work through the issues themselves.

Not only was my daughter Emma born that day, but the pregnancy super hero "Ice Chip Man" was born as well. I filled that "Ice Chip Man" role four more times over the course of the next 11 years. And no, my wife never had a working epidural during labor with any of our children. She is something else.

BASIC NOTES

- 20-25% of the population.

- Examples: Bill Gates, Stephen Hawking, Meryl Streep.

- Cs like quality answers and value.

Now that you know more about the DISC traits, you will really appreciate having your own Personality Chart. Go to The Rapport Store at: www.personalityservice.com/portal/GPPM/store.

RA TIP: We all have a unique combination of *all four* quadrants in varying degrees. These letters are not meant to box you in. Rather, they are designations to provide a starting point for you to better understand yourself and the way you see the world and communicate.

IDENTIFYING ANOTHER'S STYLE

Once you've identified your personality style, being able to recognize the DISC traits in others will make for better connections. So, while we are here, let's take a look at some of the expressed attributes for each personality style. The goal here is to make some generalizations when we are looking to understand people, in order to better connect with them.

For instance, how does each DISC style like to complete tasks?

- **D – The *Fast* Way:** They don't have time for chit chat. They want to get in and get out and onto the next task. They'll take a grocery list and literally race through the store to see if they can beat their time from last week. Now granted, they might not have thought ahead about how they were going to get through the store. They probably didn't think about putting items on their list in the order they are found in the store to maximize efficiency. That's what a C would do. :-)

- **I – The *Fun* Way:** Their first thought is "What can I do to spice this up a bit?" They're the ones who will tie dust mops to their feet and skate around the kitchen to get the floor clean. If they can't make a task fun, they're probably not going to do it.

- **S – The *Traditional* Way:** An S wants security in their activities. They believe in the motto, "If it isn't broken, don't fix it!" If they have holiday customs that were a part of their lives as children, they will be passionate about continuing those as adults with their own families.

- **C – The *Proper* Way:** What's the most efficient way to do what we're doing? Want to drive a C crazy? Take them to the mall and just browse. After about 10 minutes, here's how that conversation is going to go between two girls – one a High C and one a High I.

C: What are you looking for?

I: Nothing, really.

C: Why are we here then?

I: I just came in to look.

C: What's the point of that?

I: Just to see if there's anything cute.

C: If we do find anything cute, are you actually going to buy it?

I: I don't know. … Maybe!

C: ARRRGHH!

The C is thinking the whole time, "You go to a store to buy something. Go to the department. Try on the clothes. Pick what looks good. Pay and leave. It's pretty simple!"

Again, the I is doing things the fun way. She's outgoing and people oriented. She's just happy to be out with a friend enjoying all the different people and seeing things to try on. It's more about the experience than the end result. Neither person is wrong in thinking the way they do.

How much potential conflict is this dynamic going to be in their relationship? How much conflict could be prevented if they had the Rapport Advantage of understanding DISC? We're going to discuss avoiding unproductive conflict in a later chapter, but let's move on to Goal 3.

GOAL #3
VIEW THE WHOLE PUZZLE PICTURE

If you're having trouble deciding early on what direction a person's compass is turned, even without knowing a thing about them, lean toward people oriented. It accounts for approximately 60% of the population.

Additionally, Goals 1 and 2 have provided us with our style characteristics. Let's recap the percentages of the population for each style.

D: 10%

I: 25-30%

S: 30-35%

C: 20-25%

There are ways to determine a person's style other than having them take an assessment too. We'll discuss those later in this chapter.

Now that we understand the components of the DISC Model, the objective of Goal 3 is to provide you with some tools to quickly read people, build rapport, and increase influence – at work and in life.

CONSIDERATIONS FOR CONNECTING WITH OTHERS

In terms of personality styles, there are three main areas we need to consider before we ever speak or communicate with people with whom we want to connect.

1. What does each style *enjoy or like?*

2. What *question* does each style focus on?

3. What are the *motivators* for each style?

If we know the answers to these three questions, we can tailor our pitch/presentation/conversation to more deeply connect with each style.

WHAT DOES EACH STYLE LIKE?

We need to look at what each personality appreciates. That is, what makes them happy? What do they like? These are generalities of course. If we can appeal to these likes, it makes rapport building much easier.

- **D Likes to Win:** High D children will try to *destroy* their Grandmother at checkers. When they win, they will triumphantly get up from the table and say, "In your face Granny!" They will then begin a rehearsed victory dance for at least 10 to 15 seconds. From a business perspective, Ds are going to win. In sales, this means that a "no" is just another step on the way to a "yes." It also means they won't stop until they achieve the desired outcome. It's what I call a "bulldog" mentality. Ds won't stop until they get what they want.

- **I Likes to Be Liked:** Is enjoy being around others and being recognized for their accomplishments. The public handshake with the CEO for a job well done is a nice reward for a pure High I. They want to make others laugh and feel comfortable around them. They want to be the life of the party in social situations.

- **S Likes to Be Accepted:** Ss want to fit in. They want to be a small part of something bigger than them. Anytime they can contribute to a win for the team, they are so excited. The key to their success lies in collaboration, not isolation.

- **C Likes to Be Right:** High Cs want to get things correct. Whether it be hanging pictures in their office, the numbers in that proposal, or their child's homework, they expect things to be done the right way. "Why settle for less than your best?" I can hear my wife saying that to our second child right now.

WHAT QUESTION DOES EACH STYLE FOCUS ON?

What is the primary question each style asks when processing information? This is the ultimate question you need to have an answer for at some point in the conversation/sales process/getting to know you phase.

We'll approach this discussion from the sales perspective.

- **D Asks WHAT?** *What* are the benefits/deliverables of your offering? Ds are focused on outcomes. If I buy your product/ service:
  - What will happen?
  - What can I expect?
  - What's the bottom line?

- **I Asks WHO?** *Who* are we going to need to hire or let go? They are people focused. If I buy your product/service:
  - Who will we need to hire?
  - Who will be on the implementation team?
  - Who has the best skill set to roll this out to our company?

- **S Asks HOW?** *How* is this going to impact our current goals? It took them months to accept the *first* set of goals. They don't like change. If I buy your product/service:
  - How is this going to impact our current goals?
  - How does this affect our current product offering?
  - How do we let our customers know we're making this change?

- **C Asks WHY?** *Why* do we need this? In every situation you must have a logical answer ready.
  - Why should we make this change?
  - Why should we buy from you?
  - Why is this product better than version 2.5 that came out only 6 months ago?

WHAT MOTIVATES EACH STYLE?

We need to look at each style's basic *motivators*. What gets them "geeked" out every day to do what they need to do?

High Ds' motivators are:

- **Challenges:** They love to tackle the issues/problems that no one else knows how to solve. What other styles may see as impossible, a D's resolve says, "You just haven't tried hard enough."

- **Choices:** Give them options when they are in charge of a situation. "We can choose option A, then restart from scratch. Or, we can go with option B, go back 6 months and pick it up from there and move forward." This gives them a sense of authority.

- **Control:** Ds like being in charge. It's that simple. They want to be the decision-maker and take whatever comes – the good and the bad – from those decisions. If you have a High D on your team, put them in charge of something. You'll thank me later.

High Is' motivators are:

- **Recognition:** Publicly let them know how well they did on a project or assignment. They want to know that they are meeting or exceeding your expectations.

- **Approval:** In sales, this is a challenge. Is want to have people's approval. When a prospect says no to them, it's easy for an I to take that personally. Give them some strong coaching and let them know that a prospect isn't saying no to them. Rather, the prospect is saying no to the product/service or the timing of the offer.

- **Popularity:** Is surround themselves with people to feel better about themselves. Because they want to be liked, the more people that like them, the better off they are!

High Ss' motivators are:

- **Security:** Ss are not risk takers. They will make decisions based on preserving what they already have rather than risking that to gain something they don't currently possess. They feel safety from the consistency of a routine.

- **Appreciation:** While Is seek the limelight, Ss are fine in the shadows. Having said that, Ss need to know that they are meeting your expectations like Is do. They simply don't need, nor do they want, public praise for their efforts. A handwritten note or a quiet conversation behind closed doors telling them how much you appreciate them is a *big* motivator.

- **Assurance:** Much like with the appreciation trait, Ss like to be told that they are performing well. They take their performance evaluations very seriously. They will make changes to their behavior based on a supervisor's feedback if that feedback is given in a calm, reassuring way.

High Cs' motivators are:

- **Quality Answers:** "Because I said so" or "Because we've always done it like this" will never be a good enough answer when a High C asks "Why?" They need to know the reason behind a decision, process, or action in order to buy in. Give them the details that they need, and you will see results.

- **Excellence:** "If you're going to do it, do it right." High Cs tend to be perfectionists. They seek to be correct in everything they do. They won't settle for less than 100% in themselves or those they work with. Sometimes this means that they will take on tasks that belong to others. Their employers think, "If I give it to Carla (High C) to do, it will be completed the first time, and I won't have to go back later and fix something that someone else messed up."

- **Value:** They place a great deal of emphasis on quality. "You get what you pay for" was probably first said by a High C. They don't mind spending a bit extra on resources and tools that will help them be successful if there is an ROI (return on investment) worth the cost. They are bargain hunters, but don't like to skimp on the quality of the product.

RA TIP: The DISC Model sorts personality styles and identifies characteristics. Answering the three key questions regarding likes, questions, and motivation provides real-world applications and concrete tools.

CONFLICT AND CLARITY CHALLENGES

Before we move outside the organization to build rapport with prospects and existing clients, we need to address some of the internal challenges that we face when communicating. If we can eliminate those, we increase retention rates, build better culture, and increase overall performance. Let's re-visit the graph again (Figure 8).

Figure 8: The DISC Model of Human Behavior

Which quadrants are going to naturally have the most conflict between them? I'll give you a minute to think about it. (*Cue the game show thinking music: Ding ding dong ding ding ding dong ding ding dong ding ding ding ding ding ding ding.*)

There are two primary sources of potential conflict. If you said across the diagonals, that would be correct for one. Think about it for a moment. Diagonals are complete opposites. C: Logical, I: More illogical. D: Faster paced, S: Slower paced. I: Fun, C: Factual. S: Steady, D: Impulsive. Let's break this one down further before jumping to the second major area of conflict.

CONFLICT – ACROSS THE DIAGONALS

BETWEEN COLLEAGUES

When collaborating as a part of a team, without this DISC knowledge, conflict is sure to happen. Let's imagine we have two people from opposite diagonals working on a presentation for the company retreat. The goal is to present next year's growth projections to senior management. They have 48 hours to complete the project.

Let's start with one colleague being a High D and the other a High S. Let's see how this scenario unfolds.

> D: Okay. Let's get started. I'm going to start collecting the data. You go ahead and start e-mailing people for documentation.

> S: Wait a minute. Shouldn't we take a moment and create a plan so we know what our roles are going to be throughout the process? How are we going to know when to come back together?

> D: I'm not worried about that now. We need to get going.

S: Okay. (Sighs.)

(4 hours later)

D: Alright, where are you?

S: I've sent e-mails to four people from sales and accounting. I've only heard back from Trevor.

D: WHAT??? It's been 4 hours. Have you called them?

S: No.

D: Why not?

S: I didn't want to bother them. I'm sure they're busy.

D: We're *all* busy. *And* we have a deadline to meet.

S: Not everyone has time to drop everything they're doing for us.

D: We'll see about that. (Grabs the phone.)

Ds struggle to have patience with a High S's slower pace.

Ss are concerned about the welfare of others more than they are about their own welfare in many instances. They don't want to inconvenience other members of their team by "bothering" them with their own issues.

Ds are "take charge" personality types. In many instances, if things aren't going fast enough for them when working with an S, they will take over all aspects of a project and leave the S out. In many cases they feel like they can do it better themselves.

Unfortunately, from the S's point of view, this can create resentment and a misunderstanding of a D's true intention. In this example, the D's first priority is to make sure the project gets done. The S's priority is to not create additional tension for fellow employees by interrupting their day asking for things needed for a project that the other employees are not involved in.

Now let's look at the other diagonal – a High I and a High C. How might their initial conversation unfold?

C: Okay, what do we need to think about before we get started? What's the goal?

I: To kick butt at the retreat!!

C: Sure. … But specifically.

I: To wow people with our projections. I was thinking on slide two we could use a giraffe for the upward trend. You know, have it eating leaves, maybe in the shape of dollar bills, from a tree. It would stretch its neck really long. That would get people's attention, right?

C: We haven't even looked at all the numbers yet. What if the projections are flat?

I: Then maybe a shark. Those things are cool. You know it was Shark Week on Discovery Channel last week. On this one show, a guy was filming Great Whites and …

C: Could you focus please?

I: Sure. Big picture. Goals. Got it.

C: Did you bring the numbers?

I: I thought you were.

C: (Shakes her head.)

I live in this world constantly. Figure 9 shows you the graphs for me and my Director of Operations.

Figure 9: Personality Charts – Me and My Director of Operations

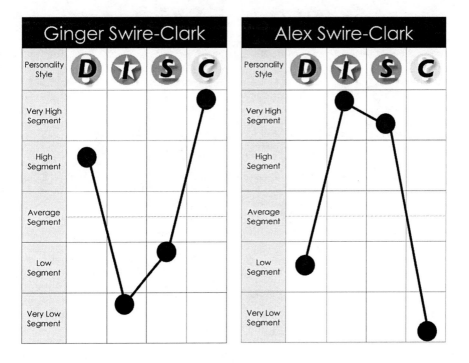

Yes, that's right. My wife and I work in the same company. We are polar opposites. She's an off-the-charts High C (100 on a 100 scale) and I am an extremely High I (100 on a 100 scale). To show it a different way, look at this circle chart that shows where we plot organizationally (Figure 10).

Figure 10: Organizational Circles – Me and My Director of Operations

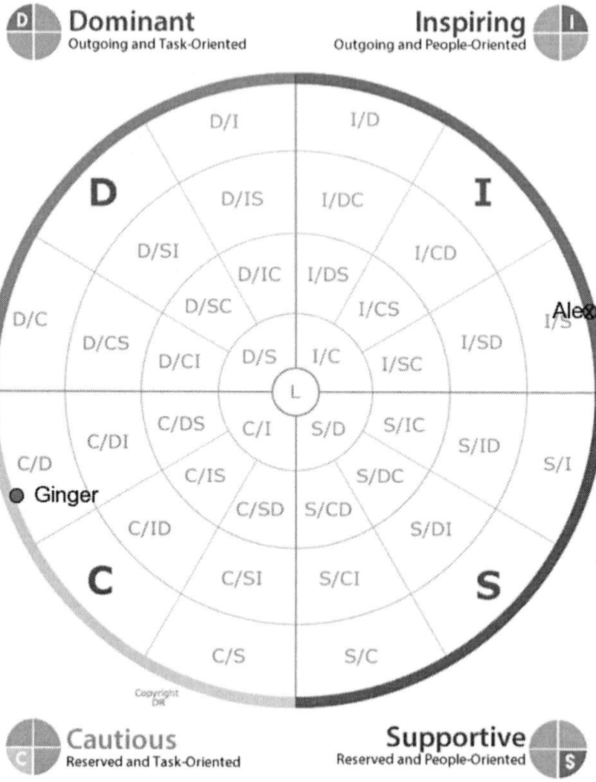
Dominant
Outgoing and Task-Oriented
Inspiring
Outgoing and People-Oriented
D
I
C
S
D/I
I/D
D/IS
I/DC
D/SI
I/CD
D/IC
I/DS
D/SC
I/CS
D/C
D/CS
D/CI
D/S
I/C
I/SC
I/SD
I/S
Alex
L
C/DS
C/I
S/D
S/IC
C/DI
S/ID
C/D
S/I
Ginger
C/IS
S/DC
C/SD
S/CD
C/ID
S/DI
C/SI
S/CI
C/S
S/C
Cautious
Reserved and Task-Oriented
Supportive
Reserved and People-Oriented

Could we be further apart?

When we're working on projects, it's like pulling teeth for her to get me to focus. She excels at big picture and process; the left side of the brain is locked in. I, on the other hand, provide the creative right side of the brain thought process and that "outside the box" thinking. High Cs are focused on the numbers. Is are focused on the look. Trying to get us to agree on how a process should flow is often tough. I generally concede on most subjects to her tremendous sense of logic and big picture thinking. I also agree with the old proverb: "Happy wife, happy life!"

RA TIP: Understanding the personality styles of those you work with, report to, and supervise will aid in creating a healthier and happier work environment for everyone.

WITHIN MANAGER-EMPLOYEE RELATIONSHIPS

Now let's imagine these diagonal style dynamics in a manager-employee relationship.

It's everyone's favorite time of year – performance reviews! Let's look at how these one-on-one debrief sessions might go based on personality styles. The manager is sitting down with the employee to discuss his/her most recent 6-month review. In these examples, we will assume that neither party has been exposed to DISC or other personality information. What happens when the manager is a High D and the employee is a High S?

> D: (Straight-faced.) Sam, your performance has been acceptable this quarter. An average of 3.5 out of 5 in all categories. Keep it up! (Walks out.)

> S: (Thinks to himself: Wait a minute. What things was I good at? Where do I need to improve? How did you come up with that score?)

There was *no* conversation, *no* exchange. For an S, this would be difficult. Ss need to know how their manager *feels* about their performance, not just what's on a graph or scoring sheet.

For Ds, they want to simply give the results. If the employee did well, great. They should want to do well already. You don't get a pat on the back for doing what you're supposed to do. They will want to move the process along quickly because they have plenty more reviews to conduct. Anything more than what needs to be said is a potential waste of time.

Can you see why there might be friction here?

Now let's reverse this same diagonal and try the same situation with a High S manager and a High D employee.

S: Come in Donna. Sit down won't you? Today, we're going to go over your evaluation. This evaluation doesn't reflect how I feel about you personally. Rather, it is about your work. If you have any questions along the way, feel free to ask them and we'll make sure we get all your questions answered before you leave.

D: (Thinking: Let's go already.)

S: Now, let's look at Question 1. "Performs tasks adequately based on the job description." You got a 3 out of 5 on that one. Would you like me to elaborate?

D: (Thinking: Not really.) Sure.

S: While you are getting your tasks done, you are not following the correct procedure every time.

D: Is the final product up to par?

S: Yes, but we're supposed to always follow steps 1 through 7 and you are consistently skipping step 6.

D: I don't see the point.

From the moment the S got started, the D was ready to walk out the door. The D knew that the process was going to take a lot longer than she wanted. Midway through the first question, the D questioned why the manager was essentially complaining about her getting her work done. As a D, she didn't understand what the problem was.

The S was focusing on making sure the D did not have any anxiety about the meeting. The S also was concerned with following a consistent procedure. Ss are all about status quo and not changing something if it is working properly. By not following the same steps every time, even though the D was producing the end result, there is anxiety on the S's part to make sure that everyone in the department was following the same procedures every time.

You could also see that if not coached well, a D could easily run over a High S manager. The S typically doesn't move as fast as the D would like them to in terms of pace of meetings, making decisions, etc. The D could see this as timidity or lack of authority and, therefore, perhaps not take the S seriously.

Ss are about feelings and showing their team members that they care and that they, as individuals, are a part of something bigger. A D isn't interested in feelings. They are more interested in getting things done.

What happens when we use the other diagonal – High I manager and High C employee? Will this go better?

> I: Carla! You did SOOOOOO awesome on your review this quarter. Hit me up top!! (Extends hand for a high five. Carla simply looks up with an "Are you serious?" look on her face). Your numbers are fantastic. Keep this up and I'll have to brag on you in front of the entire department!
>
> C: So what were my scores exactly?
>
> I: Lots of 4s and 5s!! You did great!

C: Why did I get a 4 on "Performs tasks adequately based on the job description?" I've always gotten 5s in the past when Kim did my evaluations.

I: I'm not really sure. I was just going down the list and put 4s where I thought you were good and 5s where I thought you were fantabulous!!

C: (Blank stare.)

This did not go well for the High C.

Cs are creatures of detail and facts. You can't give them an evaluation and then not give specific details on why they did or did not perform.

In this example, the High I was just so excited that the High C did well that he/she glossed over the details. To the High C, this evaluation was a waste of time. There were no facts, no constructive criticisms, and no ways to improve in order to change the 4s into 5s. A High I would not understand why the High C was staring at them blankly. After all, the High I was delivering great news. It was a job well done.

But here's the rub: High Cs always strive for perfection. When you don't give them the tools to improve any missteps that they make, it's like they are hearing nails on a chalkboard. Even worse, if you can't provide proof that there were mistakes, they will assume they should have had all 5s.

Now you have a potentially sticky HR situation.

Again, let's reverse this diagonal and see what happens. We have a High C manager and a High I employee.

C: Good afternoon Ivan. We're going to be spending an hour going over your evaluation today. Our goals for today's session are pretty straightforward. Number one, to make sure you know what parts of the job you're doing correctly. Number two, to make sure you know where your deficiencies are. Number three, to give you strategies to improve your areas of weakness. Do you have any questions before we begin?

I: Not really. I hope I did well!

C: Now, let's look at Question 1. "Performs tasks adequately based on the job description." You got a 3 out of 5 on this category. I've written here, "lack of attention to details." An example I listed is the product invoicing process. Sometimes you get all of the invoices sent out within the first 3 days. Some months, you don't send out invoices for 2 to 3 weeks after the order. The policy clearly says that "invoices should be sent to the customer with 72 hours." Why are you having difficulty following that procedure?

I: I'm not sure. Sometimes things happen.

C: Things happen? (Puzzled look.)

I: Yeah, like last week, for example. I meant to get the invoices out, but our boss Bob asked me to help organize the monthly company lunch outing. You know Bob *loves* the lunch outing, so I thought I should get that done first.

C: Organizing the company lunch isn't in your job description.

I: Yeah, but Bob needed me to get that done for him. And, that's so much more engaging than getting those invoices out.

C: (Frowns. Head is going to explode.)

It's simply about order versus chaos.

The C is all about order and a logical process for everything in their lives. The I suffers from shiny object syndrome (SOS). They can start a task, and 15 minutes into it they will move on to something else without completing the first task they started. Then they may go to a third task and then a fourth and then back to task one with no rhyme or reason.

A C is a list maker by nature and works their list typically in order of importance and urgency from top to bottom. High Is do not like monotonous tasks such as sending invoices. If there is any chance they might have to do something more enjoyable instead, they are off to the races. It's not that they can't focus, they just need a little more guidance and hand-holding than the other styles.

In all of the examples above, we have two main sources of potential issues for diagonal styles.

- **Pace**: Ds and Is are outgoing and move fast. Ss and Cs take things more slowly.

  The outgoing people want the more reserved people to hurry up. "Let's go!" "Have you had enough time to think about it because we need to make something happen?"

  The reserved people want the outgoing people to slow it down. "Hang on a minute. Let's think this through. Why are we in such a hurry? We need to consider all of our options."

- **Compass**: As we mentioned in Goal 1, we all have a compass that points us to being more task oriented or people oriented. The left side of the graph is all about details. The right side is about relationships.

When you have a D – fast paced and task oriented – working with an S – slower paced and people oriented – you end up with predictable arguments.

D: Why can't you move faster?

S: What's the hurry? Have we considered other options?

D: Of course. And besides, I've got other things to get done.

S: So do I. You don't need to get bent out of shape. Besides, I'm not sure you've thought this through.

D: What makes you say that?

S: Remember the last time you "went with your gut?"

D: (Stares in anger.)

RA TIP: To be more successful in these situations, both parties need to adapt emotionally. They need to meet in the middle from where they normally behave. We will give you some insight and tips on emotional adaptation a little later.

CONFLICT – WITHIN THE SAME QUADRANT

Conflict can also occur with two or more personalities from the same quadrant. Three of the four quadrants have some potential landmines to navigate when it comes to conflict.

- **More Than One D:** Two Ds want to be in charge. If they are in the same group, they most likely want to both be head honcho. To alleviate this potential issue, give them each something that they are responsible for/assigned to where they have autonomy in terms of how the work is done. This will give them great incentive to achieve and show you what they are made of. Again, as we said earlier, put a D in charge of people or a process and they will be successful. Put one D in charge of a process on the project and let the other D be in charge of other people on the project as general oversight.

- **Two Is:** Wait. Seriously? Aren't they all about having fun? Well, sure they are. The only potential issue here is avoiding competitive jousting. One High I may make a joke in a meeting. Later, the other I might pull a gag to top the last joke, get the bigger laugh. Many Is aren't comfortable in their own skin and use humor as a defense mechanism. Give each I a chance to shine in their own way and you will have a lifelong fan.

- **More Than One C:** This one should be pretty obvious. We already said that Cs are never wrong. Put two Cs together and they are going to battle to determine who is correct. They will provide a steady stream of facts and numbers to support their individual ideas. Sometimes, the best way for them to collaborate is to have them work independently first to come up with a solution, making sure they document their sources. Then, they both bring their information to the table and present it to the rest of the group. The most factual support should win out!

Inside your organization, it's a bit easier to get everyone on the same page. Just bring me in to talk to your group! Ha! Seriously, you can shape your company's culture and communication by educating everyone on these concepts. DISC will help your teams be more cohesive and improve morale over all. A more difficult move comes when you need to go outside your organization to exert influence and build relationships. This next section provides tips on building rapport with those you don't know as well.

RULES FOR BUILDING RAPPORT FOR NEW PROSPECTS/PEOPLE

Before we start down this road, I want to make sure we lay down some ground rules when building rapport with others and using your new-found DISC powers.

1. **Care for the Person's Well-being.** We should always use our DISC information to improve the lives of others.

2. **Be Genuine.** No one is asking you to change who you are. We are suggesting that if you use this information to help reach people, with the goal of helping achieve their goals and dreams, you'll be genuinely yourself even though you are adapting your behavior. Think of it very loosely like the scene from the movie *Hitch*, where Will Smith plays the role of a matchmaker trying to help Kevin James' character, Albert, get noticed by a beautiful heiress, Allegra. Hitch gives Albert a tip to create a moment of "shock and awe" so that she will notice him. During a financial advisory meeting for Allegra, Albert, though timid at first, stands up to his superior and then takes it to the next level, quitting his job and walking out of the boardroom. She later admits that she wouldn't have noticed him without that shock and awe moment. From a rapport building standpoint, we're not looking for shock and awe. We're looking for ways to connect with people quickly and meaningfully so when the conversation is over, the other person says, "That was a great conversation," or "What a nice guy," or "I think I can trust her."

3. **Use Your DISC Powers for Good.** Going back to number 1 on this list, we should use these tools to help others. If we benefit, that is great! But we should *never* use these tools to manipulate someone to do what we want them to do for our own benefit. Used properly in a personal relationship, DISC can have life-changing positive effects. My marriage has been all the better for it. If someone were using it to manipulate another

person, that person has now become an emotional leech, taking instead of giving in a full and free way. To paraphrase what Master Yoda said to Luke Skywalker in *The Empire Strikes Back*, "If anger you use to win, a dark road it will take you on." Don't use your DISC knowledge to get back at someone or just to get something you want.

Now that we understand the rules we should follow, the primary drivers of each style, and the main questions to consider when connecting with others, let's look at ways that we can read people's styles.

THREE POINTS TO POWERFUL RELATIONSHIPS

We can't start every conversation with, "Hey Sally! What DISC style are you?" If it were only that easy. I have a three-step process for building the foundation of rapport, including actions to take before you ever meet someone! If you follow these steps you will have the tools to make a great first impression and create lightning quick connections with others. I call it the Three Points to Powerful Relationships.

1. Analyze correspondence

2. Explore social media and identify commonalities

3. Observe in person and use your DISC knowledge to analyze the data

1. ANALYZE CORRESPONDENCE

People can convey their style through their writing. You can use that information to begin building rapport before you even meet or speak to them!

In this scenario, let's say you sent an e-mail that asked, "Did you get the proposal I sent over yesterday?" Below is what a typical response from each style would look like and your best response for a good connection.

———————

D: Yes. Will be in touch.

Short, to the point. They are not going to discuss it in that moment or offer additional comments. You asked a yes or no question and they answered it. Case closed.

In most cases, you'll want to mirror their communication style. This will make them comfortable and feel at ease as the conversation goes back and forth.

You: Excellent. Thanks.

———————

I: Yes thanks. I'm excited to read it and see what you offer. :-)

Expresses energy. Is struggle with e-mail not allowing them to show their feelings. E-mail is a cold medium. They want to make sure the message recipient knows exactly the tone they wish to convey. That's why you'll see the use of emoticons (even in business correspondence) or lots of exclamation points!!!!!

You: Excellent! I look forward to your response.

———————

S: Sorry I didn't get back to you. I've been quite busy. Thanks for sending it. I hope to get back to you tomorrow.

Ss want to be supportive and don't want to offend. They will be anxious that the sender might be concerned that it has been over 24 hours since the proposal arrived. Often, they will be almost apologetic in their tone when responding.

You: It's no rush. Take your time. I look forward to your response.

C: Yes. I am looking over the document on Thursday morning. I will return it to you with my comments in light blue highlighting. You should hear back from me by 1 p.m. EST on that day.

WHOA! Information overload. Cs will give you exact details of their response to ensure clarity. They don't want anything to be misunderstood or for things to fall through the cracks.

You: Very good. Let me know if you have any additional questions.

2. EXPLORE SOCIAL MEDIA AND IDENTIFY COMMONALITIES

Let me start this section by saying we're looking to make connections between you and the other person that allow you to have a meaningful conversation on a topic. There are three ways this happens.

1. Discovering shared interests

2. Discovering shared rivalries/dislikes

3. Discovering what they enjoy

We will break down each of these scenarios by exploring social media.

On LinkedIn you can find out a tremendous amount about people's passions. At the bottom of their profile under "Interests" you can see the things they support that may or may not be business related. This includes charities they support. At the time of this writing there is a separate volunteer section that affords insight into where they spend their time giving back to the community. Here we are looking for shared interests that create easy conversation or we are being genuinely curious about something they're involved in.

You might say, "I saw on LinkedIn that you support Tanner's Totes. I've never heard of it. Can you tell more about it?" Most likely they will go into a monologue about the cause, describing why they are so passionate about it. (If they don't tell you the reason behind the passion, *ask*!!)

"Go Tar Heels!!" After my shout out, you had one of three reactions.

1. Yeah baby! Love those basketball Heels!! 2017 National Champs!!!

2. Tar Heels? Seriously?? I hate those fans. Bunch of wine and cheese losers in Chapel Hill!

3. I'm not that big into sports.

Any of those three responses opens a door for you to deepen the conversation.

1. **Shared Interest:** I know, right!?! Did you go to school there?

2. **Shared Rivalry:** We're not all that bad. So let me guess, Duke or State fan?

3. **What They Enjoy:** Oh yeah? What are you a big fan of? They might say movies, gardening, board games, charity work. Who knows? It doesn't matter what topic they are interested in. From there you can ask them more about whatever "it" is to get a genuine understanding of the topic and see if there are any additional commonalities that you share.

The same principles apply for hobbies and causes. You can get a good sense of a person's hobbies as they post pictures of their projects and pastimes on Pinterest. While Facebook also provides information through pictures, people will often share a post dealing with a subject that interests them or they're passionate about. Remember how many times the picture of the big-game hunter dentist was shared in 2015? Here are some examples of openings to get you started.

For a shared interest, you can lead with, "I liked the picture of your birthday cake on Pinterest."

Them: Yeah, I love baking and decorating.

You: Me too! Do you make any other specialty cakes?

———◆———

For a shared rivalry/dislike, you might start with, "I saw on Facebook that you are anti-chess."

Them: Yeah, I never understood why so many people play it.

You: I don't do very well at it either. Thank goodness there are so many other cool games to choose from. Do you play other games?

———◆———

If you are trying to determine what they enjoy from a post, begin with something like, "I saw on LinkedIn that you support the March of Dimes 5K Run for Babies. Are you a runner?"

Them: No, I don't like running. It hurts my knees.

You: I only run when I'm being chased! So why do you support the cause?

———◆———

Snapchat and Instagram are very visual platforms. There are tons of pictures on a variety of topics on both. In Snapchat, simply use the search tool to look for a topic that you have an interest in such as "podcast." "Publisher stories" will appear that feature podcasts and podcast topics. Speak directly to those creators for conversation starters.

For Instagram, use the magnifying glass to search for any type of hashtag on an interest from a potential ICA (Ideal Client Avatar) to then start a conversation. You can even follow a hashtag if you want to keep up with activity related to the topic for which you created the hashtag.

There are no dead ends in this format if you ask questions that are based on *genuine* curiosity. Again, we are in the infant stages of trying to build relationships.

The key is to ask questions that engage more than a one-word response.

> **Disclaimer:** We are making connections here, not stalking. You want to show interest, not give people the heebie-jeebies. You don't need to tell people you know what hospital in which they were born.

3. OBSERVE IN PERSON AND USE DISC KNOWLEDGE TO ANALYZE THE DATA

My office desk is one big pile of insanity. Sticky notes here, earbuds over there. I can find all my things but no one else can. My Director of Operations is the opposite. Everything has its proper place. Things are color coded, alphabetized. There's method without the madness.

We reveal our different personality styles through various clues without needing an assessment – the way we dress, the way we talk, the way our offices look, our body language.

RA TIP: Don't simply use one of these tools and then think, "Look at this office, she's totally a High C." She might be brand new to the company and hasn't had a chance to personalize her office yet. Use all of these tools (both the "pre-in-person" tools above as well as the "once you've met them" tools below) in tandem to get the best overall picture of what style they are.

OFFICE DECOR

For this section, in addition to giving you things to look for, I'll give you engagement questions that you can use to dive deeper and get a great feel for their style.

D: Large desk, awards, useful accessories

Engagement question: (Looking at degrees/awards/plaques) "Which of those are you most proud of?"

This is a great question to have out of curiosity. It also shows that you have interest in something that's obviously meaningful to them. When we ask this question, we are appealing to their ego. For Ds, their ego is what drives them to be successful.

———————

I: Flashy, trendy, with fun pictures

Engagement question: "That's a cool picture. Where was that taken?"

Smile and sincerely be engaged. Once they mention the place, actively listen. Once they have finished, take a moment to think about any connections you might have to that place. Maybe you've been there before. Maybe someone you know has been there. Mention these ideas with a leading question, such as "What was your favorite part of that trip/experience/moment?"

———

S: Family pictures, personal mementos

Engagement question: "That's a _____ family. How old are they?"

If you have kids/nieces/nephews, find a similar age and then find a similar experience. Ask about what grade they are going into. What activities are they involved in?

———

C: Aesthetically pleasing, unique, functional

Engagement question: "This office looks amazing! How do you keep it so organized?"

Other personality styles might consider High Cs to be "neat freaks." Organization is not a bad thing. Compliment them on the way their area looks. Then you could offer some self-deprecating humor about your office looking like a pig sty. That will get them to chuckle or smile and ease any tension or anxiety they may be having.

BODY LANGUAGE

- **D – Big Gestures, Leans Forward, Advancing:** Mirroring with Ds is often necessary. If you don't match them, they can see it as weakness and that creates distance between you.

- **I – Expressive, Friendly Posture, Amusing:** Let them have the stage and be an attentive listener. Ask more questions to help them keep going.

- **S – Gentle Gestures, Reassuring:** Take things slowly. Ask questions about family, friends, etc. Nothing controversial.

- **C – Unemotional, Controlled Gestures, Assessing:** It can sometimes be difficult to get Cs to elaborate. Ask questions about why they do what they do or why they chose to work for the company/firm.

VOICE: SPEECH PATTERN AND TONE

- **D – Directive Tones, Abrupt, Interrupting, Intentional:** Ds are often misjudged. Their desire to get things done quickly can be perceived as rudeness. This is especially true for Ss and Cs. Remember, Ds are doers. They are looking to get as many things done as quickly as possible. When making a point, if you start with, "Let me tell you a story," they are most likely to roll their eyes and begin drumming their fingers. They simply want you to "Land your plane!!" They will speak quickly and concisely. To build rapport, match them in this regard.

- **I – Talkative, Varied Tones, Personal, Easily Distracted:** Is love to talk about themselves. Their enthusiasm is almost endless. They will talk to a stop sign if they think the big red octagon is listening! They get excited when they find mutual connections in others. However, they have shiny object syndrome (SOS). Don't be upset with them if you are meeting in a public place and they glance up to see if they know anyone else there, or they look up at a TV in a sports bar every few seconds. It's difficult for them to focus for long periods of time.

- **S – Conversational, Warm Tones, Friendly, Prefers Listening:** Ah, the Ss, such great listeners. Their warm smiles and easy laughs make conversations go so smoothly. When you want a sympathetic ear, seek out an S. They'd much rather listen than dominate the conversation. And once you're done laying out the problem or the frustrations of your day, their keen understanding of the feelings of others can provide tremendous insight. This is especially true if your style is located on the task (left) side of the graph.

- **C – Clarifying, Monotone, Logical, Focused, Questioning:** Having a conversation with a High C can be challenging at times. In group discussions, they sit, often stone-faced, taking in everyone's opinions and the facts regarding the situation, never once adding their own opinion to the discussion. They see the world as one process after another that can be improved. From the way the check-out line moves at a grocery store to how a highway's on and off ramp system could be more streamlined, Cs see things that can be improved. Nothing is ever perfect. As we said earlier, they are constantly asking why? Their brains are always on, thinking of the process but oftentimes not the people involved.

ATTIRE

- **D – Power Suit, Impressive Accessories:** The classic power suit. For men, clean and crisp. No frills tie. For women, business suit, monochromatic. Look for large class rings, big watches, signs of success.

- **I – Expressive, Fun:** Flashy suits. Fun ties and accessories. Conversation-starting earrings or other jewelry.

- **S – Comfort Over Flare:** They will be the least noticeable person in the room. Muted colors and little jewelry. Nothing controversial.

- **C – Function, Function, Function:** Some stereotypes are based in a hint of truth. For example, look at 80s movies. If you wanted an actor to play a "geek" or "nerd," the standard costume included thick glasses and a pocket protector on their button down shirt. This pocket protector had pens and other tools to help the character accomplish his/her goals. It was functional.

  In today's society, the term "geek" is lauded. "Life hacks" are created by self-proclaimed "neat geeks." Best Buy's service team has geek in its name. Today's Cs aren't wearing pocket protectors. They are, however, not as concerned with how people view them as other styles might be. They are wearing clothes that don't get in the way of the execution of their daily tasks. In the business sector, they consider a suit to be a uniform of sorts. They will consistently wear the same few outfits repeatedly because they don't need to try anything else if what they have works.

Understanding yourself is the first and sometimes most difficult step. We have parents, friends, significant others who, throughout our lives and in good faith, often try to shape us into people more like them. They have good intentions but ultimately are missing this methodology. If they understood these concepts they would be more accepting of who you are and embrace the mindset that it's perfectly natural for you to be who you are and not like them.

Understanding what other personality types like and what motivates them allows us to clarify any conflicts between our styles and build a connection. We must learn to work with people in our organizations, even if we are in opposite quadrants, or in some cases the same quadrant. Often the people on our team are simply the people we have to learn about, connect, and build a rapport with. Additionally, new prospects and people come into our lives almost every day. We can cultivate those relationships using the Three Points to Powerful Relationships.

With a little insight into outlining the key personality tendencies and filling that in with the four personality quadrants, we come to understand ourselves and others while building rapport for more meaningful connections.

And with that we've completed the three goals. Yee-hah!! But I promised if you stayed with me I'd give you a bonus – some techniques specifically aimed at workplace adaptations and benchmarking. You made it, so turn the page for your bonus!

BONUS GOAL
EMOTIONAL ADAPTATION AND MORE

WHY IS ADAPTING EMOTIONALLY SO DIFFICULT?

We have our normal style that is most comfortable to us – our own "happy place" if you will. That is your basic style. I am a High I/S style. This means that out of a scoring range of 1-100, with 100 being the highest, both my I and S are above 50. See my graph (as a review) in Figure 11.

My I is 100 and my S is 92. Any style quadrant (D, I, S, or C) that scores above 50 on the assessment is a predominant style. Make sense? The opposite of that is true as well. Any quadrant less than 50 is a trait that is not expressed to a significant degree, and therefore is not a trait that we are naturally comfortable in or drawn toward.

Earlier, we spoke about the "midline." The midline occurs at 50 on the graph. Another name for this line could be the energy line (see Figure 11). Any trait exhibited above this line does not require you to adapt for that particular style. You do not use additional energy. Any trait below that line requires a great deal of emotional adapting – mental and emotional energy.

Figure 11: Alex's Personality Chart

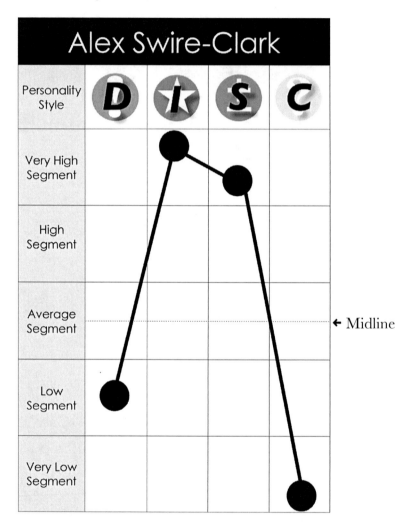

There are two ways that we adapt emotionally on a daily basis: internally and externally. We've touched on external adapting in Goal 3. External emotional adapting happens when two people of different styles communicate or work together. Internal adapting occurs when we are challenged to look at things from another style's perspective.

EXTERNAL ADAPTING

In external adapting, we discussed that there are many instances when you need to meet in the middle between two different styles. The most challenging adapting comes when diagonally opposite styles are communicating or working together – Ds with Ss; Is with Cs.

If Ds are hard charging all the time, the Ss are most likely not going to engage and will have large amounts of anxiety. They will be looking to exit your organization ASAP if they are continually working with a D that goes unchecked. If Ss can't make decisions and move forward when challenges arise, the Ds will feel handcuffed and will take over responsibilities that are outside their job description just to get them done, and then they will be chastised by their supervisor for "not following the rules." Guess who's looking for the exit now?

When Is are involved in a project, they can become easily distracted even if they do high quality work in the end. Cs get terribly frustrated with this and can't figure out how to keep them on task. The Is can't understand why the High Cs don't lighten up a bit. A High I might think, "Why are you so serious all the time?" In either case, both parties are frustrated.

Each style is frustrated by the completely different behaviors being exhibited by other styles. We haven't talked about things such as missing a quota, showing up late for work, excessive use of profanity, or any other outside factor that could cause frustration. We're merely talking about behaviors that are exhibited by a person's basic personality style.

If each person on your team (or in your family) had this DISC knowledge and could apply it effectively, how much better would your culture be? How much would your turnover rates drop? The key is *application and consistent education*. It's not simply understanding who you are. It doesn't stop with understanding other people's styles. The key is adapting.

With internal adaptation, a person is challenged by his/her own view of the world. A High C, for example, will have to break out of the world of *order* to understand the chaotic world of an I style. Again, the same thought keeps popping up: Not everyone sees the world the same way as you do. Not everyone thinks the same way as you. Each style has its own individual adapting hurdles to jump over on a daily basis. More on internal adapting in just a bit.

RA TIP: DISC knowledge shows us where to adapt. But more than this, internal adaptation requires us to look inward, to be self-aware. External adaptation involves empathy, being aware of and sensitive to the feelings, thoughts, and experiences of another.

TIPS FOR SUCCESSFUL EMOTIONAL ADAPTING

What does each style need to understand that will make adapting a bit easier?

Each style is handcuffed by its weaknesses. Cs tend to see the world in black and white and absolutes, struggling with flexibility. Ss tend to be resistant to change. They fear new processes and perhaps people they haven't encountered before. Is tend to get off track and occasionally let their need for fun affect their sense of judgment. Ds tend to be on full speed all the time. They struggle to slow down to the people around them.

As we look at this next section, I'm not trying to call anyone out. I'm certainly not trying to be negative. I want to point out things you need to understand to be the best *you* that you can be.

Here are five things Ds need to know.

1. **People Are Important.** It's not always about getting things done as fast as humanly possible. You're going to end up stepping on people along the way. Those relationships may not seem important in the moment but, you may do some things you regret later. Take time to listen to others. Have a casual conversation around the water cooler or coffee pot. If people know, like, and trust you, they are more likely to follow and support you.

2. **Relaxation Is Not a Crime.** As we used to say back in the 80s, "Take a Chill Pill man!" or as my 13-year-old son would say now, "Hold up, bruh!!" Life is a journey and we should enjoy the trip. Not everyone is driven to get results the same way you are. Seek to understand how others around you define success. It may not require the 14-hour day regimen that you place on yourself.

3. **Some Controls Are Necessary.** The High Ds "just get it done" mentality can have its consequences. Even if you don't agree with procedures, you should follow them. I'm not telling you to follow them blindly. When you do question the origins and rationale of processes with others, do so in a respectful tone and with well-thought-out reasoning. Don't simply fly off the handle, burst into your supervisor's office and demand a change. If you're dealing with an S or C style, that will have the opposite effect that you intend.

4. **Everyone Has a Boss.** Yes, that includes you too! Whether it is a manager, the CEO, or the police officer who said you were going 20 miles over the speed limit when she pulled you over, we all have to answer to someone. Be respectful of authority. Also remember when you are in a position of authority, be respectful to those you are leading.

5. **Expressing Your Conclusions Helps Others Understand Them Better.** As we said earlier, every style processes information by asking specific questions. Who, how, and why are being asked by the I, S, and C in your organization. If you present a new initiative without rationale or elaboration, you will *not* get buy in. Take the time to formulate your reasoning. Present it in an easy-to-understand format. Then, be prepared to be asked questions. Don't mistake the questions as challenging you or the initiative. Rather, your colleagues have different styles for seeking clarification so that they can fully understand and then support what you have conveyed.

Here are the five things Is need to know.

1. **Time Must Be Managed.** With so many different things that need to get done during the day it's tough for Is to stay focused. Get a planner. Use a task tracking app. People will expect you to get things done, and on time. Find some tools that can help and you'll be organized *and* fun to be around!

2. **Too Much Optimism Can Be Harmful.** Is have a natural "glass half full" mentality about most things. This is great when inspiring others, when people are looking for hope. However, if you're Sally Sunshine all of the time, it can be a bit annoying. One example that comes to mind is when you are interviewing candidates for a position in your company. If a candidate comes in and has a great sense of humor, you're sold! Résumé, shmesume. With that cheerful attitude, this candidate can accomplish anything! You become their champion based on your first impression without looking at the data. It's okay to be critical and slow down a bit when making decisions. Your team will thank you for it.

3. **Listening Is Important.** Is like to express themselves, *a lot*. So much so that when they are in a conversation with someone else, by the time five words are out of the other person's mouth,

High Is have their response ready to go, sometimes tuning out the rest of what the other person is saying. Be an active listener, repeat what the other person has said to gain clarity. Focus on them. Mirror their body language. Use empathy. Pay attention to details. You will earn people's trust this way.

4. **Tasks Must Be Completed.** Yes, I know. You're *not* task oriented. I get that. There is still work to be done. Whether it's getting that presentation finished before 8 a.m. tomorrow, or getting all ten of the items on the grocery list, people need to know they can count on you. Again, use tools to help you plan your day and week so that you can stay organized. Get your most difficult tasks done early in the day. That way, you can build in more flexibility in the afternoon.

5. **Accountability Is Imperative.** Mike Scott of totallyaccountable.com defines accountability as, "Doing *what* you said you'd do, *as* you said you would do it, *when* you said you would do it – *period*." For Is that means no excuses. Get it done. For exercise purposes, many use an accountability partner, like a personal trainer. If you need an accountability partner in business, seek out a High C who can help you work on knocking out those details. You can help them learn to enjoy the simple moments in life.

Ss need to know these five things.

1. **Change Provides Opportunity.** Nothing ever stays the same. As an organization, you're either getting better or worse. Be flexible when change happens. Analyze the change, ask questions if you need to. Embrace it. Give the change an opportunity to be fully realized. If there is a new policy put into place, don't go over the deep end on day one or two when

the transition is still evolving. Give the policy, and yourself, a chance to react and respond. It will all be okay.

2. **Friendship Isn't Everything.** When we are in the workplace, we have friends there of course. As Ss, more than any other style, we value those relationships. However, we can't let those friendships cloud our judgment in terms of what is right and wrong, and what we're supposed to be doing on a daily basis. Friends enter and leave our lives along the journey. Don't sacrifice your principles to continue a friendship that may be unhealthy.

3. **Discipline Is Good.** Much like the High I, High Ss struggle with discipline as well. Only Ss struggle from a standpoint of "over helping" others. We see this happen with people in our organization from time to time. Someone in the department has an issue or problem. Here comes High S Stacy to save the day. Stacy will do research, come up with solutions, and collect website information with her resources. She is there to help. The person with the original problem is always very appreciative. But wait. How long did that "I'll be helpful" project take Stacy? Was that part of her job description? If not, then she hasn't been doing what she was hired to do. Now, she might have to stay over and finish up those tasks that are her normal responsibility. If this is chronic, it can be detrimental to her work mindset, her family life, etc. Stay focused on your job responsibilities. You have to help yourself first before you can help others.

4. **It Is Okay to Say "No."** No one is going to get mad at you. You're most likely not going to lose friendships. There's only one of you with so many hours in the day. Prioritize the work you need to get done. Then, if there is time to help others, knock yourself out!

5. **Being a Servant Doesn't Mean Being a "Sucker."** It's pretty obvious by now that High Ss love to be supportive and help others. Don't get caught in the trap of being the "Mikey" of your organization. Back in the early 70s Life cereal introduced a commercial where two young kids were given a bowl of new cereal that was supposed to be "good for you." The first says, "I'm not going to try it." The second says, "Well, I'm not going to try it." Then the first kid has an idea, "Let's get Mikey. Yeah." He pushes the bowl in front of Mikey who is clearly the younger sibling. Mikey, trusting his older sibling, begins to eat the cereal. Now, in the end, Mikey ends up liking the cereal, but that is not the point. The point was that Mikey, as a younger sibling, was a "yes man." His older brother offered, so he said yes. As we get older and become more self-aware, we should be able to say no to things that aren't morally right, require too much time, are outside the scope of our work, or don't fit with our beliefs. It's okay to say no. You'll thank yourself in the long run when you learn to use this simple word.

Finally, Cs need to know these five things.

1. **Total Agreement Isn't Always Necessary.** You're going to make a persuasive argument based on tons of research and data. You've got the evidence to support your conclusions. It all looks great. Then someone says, "I get what you're saying, but something just doesn't feel right." *Feel?* You're saying no based on your feelings??? Yes, indeed. Thousands of business decisions over the years have been based on a gut feeling or a hunch. Understand that not everyone is as fact driven as you are. Leave some room for the emotional part of any decision.

2. **Thorough Explanations Are Not Always Possible.** Your need to know why in all situations sometimes just isn't doable. If you're creating a new product line that has never hit the market before, it's going to be hard to do projections. Sure, you can look at similar products. However, sometimes you're going to

have to accept, "We've made a decision to discontinue this line of services. We just didn't feel like the market would support it in five years. That's all we're comfortable saying at this time." Your charts clearly show a steady increase in sales over the last few years. However, the CEO's stance is the CEO's stance. Grit your teeth and move on. The CEO already has.

3. **Deadlines Must Be Met.** Hang on a second. Didn't we say just a few pages ago that accountability is imperative for the High Is? High Cs don't have that problem. They're conscientious, pragmatic – *stop*! That's correct. However, High Cs live on the opposite end of that spectrum. You don't miss deadlines because you lack focus. You miss deadlines because the work isn't perfect. Yes, I'm playing the perfectionist card. You want to make 100% sure that the data matches your analysis without any holes in logic. High Cs want the charts to be color coded in ROYGBIV order. The outline of the presentation has to be in the standardized font. The PowerPoint has to be exactly right, so much so that you've run through the same unedited slide deck 30 times to make sure everything is just as it should be. Sometimes, 98% is good enough. Especially when you're on a tight schedule. Give it your best effort in the time that you have and then go with it. Life doesn't give us infinite extensions. There's a beginning and an end; so too it is with our work on projects.

4. **Taking a Calculated Risk Can Be Profitable.** This goes back to the point we made in number one. The numbers tell High Cs what they should do. It's all about the math. If the numbers make sense, move forward. If they don't, we drop/ change the plan. For Ds and Is, it's less about the numbers and more about "a feeling." Understand, that people will say, "I understand what the numbers are saying, but …" The future is a fickle thing. Worthy calculated risks are based on a bit of the numbers and the gut.

5. **There Are Varying Degrees of Excellence.** For High Cs, it's 100% or bust. I had a High C friend in high school who cried in class when she found out she received 97 on a test. Are you kidding me? I would have been doing the cabbage patch and the running man up and down the back of the classroom. (High I sidenote: The cabbage patch and running man were 80s dance moves. I was quite the little dancing machine back in the day!!) We all define excellence in our own way. Try to understand other people's definition when you are working with them rather imposing your standards upon them. I can tell you from experience, it is hard to live up to a High C's definition of excellence.

INTERNAL ADAPTING

When you go to work, oftentimes you'll put on your "emotional mask." You are putting on the style that you think your workplace/job description requires. This is your adapting style. It could be similar to your basic style.

For example, a natural High I who is in sales will have an adapting style graph very similar to his/her basic graph. However, a High I who works in accounting where there are lots of numbers, facts, and figures to analyze on a daily basis would not lead with their I trait, but would rather need to channel his/her C style. If that person's basic style has a C score that is a pathetic 4, like mine, it will take a great deal of adapting – energy – to get to the point where he/she is at or above the midline.

Adapting is draining. As CEO and a High I, my least favorite time of the month is the end of the month. I've got put P&L statements together, look at forecasting, analyze our trailing 12- and 24-month numbers. Those are all High C kinds of tasks. Go ahead and kick me in the shin and give me a root canal at the same time. I can spend an hour doing those tasks and to me it will feel like I spent 8 hours digging a trench. Again, each trait is measured on a 1-100 scale. The tiny C in my graph is a 4. So I have to move 46 points just to get to the midline to perform C tasks at an average level. If I have to create a high level of detail in those tasks I need to go higher up, past the midline. I am wiped out when those tasks are finished, even if they don't take very long.

The flip side of that would be when I'm speaking to corporations or associations. Put me on the stage in front of 500 people talking to them about emotional intelligence and how they can save wounded relationships – I'm in heaven. I could do that all day every day!! If a High C had to get up in front of a group of ten people and speak to those people every day to try to motivate them, they would experience the same effects that I do from invoicing. They would be adapting emotionally and it would cause them great angst and fatigue because they would use so much energy to channel a very High I skill. They can't stand going to their polar opposite style. Can they do it? Absolutely! Should they continue to do that on a daily basis if they want to remain sane? Definitely not.

Question: What types of activities in the workplace cause each style to exert a significant amount of emotional adaptation?

- D: Showing empathy, slowing down their internal motor, working as a team

- I: Doing very detailed process work, multi-tasking, working on projects that do the same thing over and over

- S: Confronting others, constantly changing roles, making quick decisions

- C: Working with others, designing creative activities, giving pep talks

Again, it's not that each style *can't* do those actions successfully (e.g., a D showing empathy), it simply takes a massive amount of energy to execute those actions successfully. The lower your trait is in that area (a

High D with an S score of 10 or less trying to have empathy), the more challenging it will be.

COSTS OF ADAPTING

If people come to work day after day, emotionally adapting in their current role, two things will happen: burnout and turnover. They will not stay at their current employer if they are required to constantly adapt emotionally. Their sense of fulfillment is diminished, and they question why they are even there.

Imagine a High S who has to fire people on a weekly basis or a High C who has to get on the phone every day and answer questions from customers. The High I who has to produce daily productivity spreadsheets or the High D who is forced to work with others on group projects who are painfully slow.

Now some of you may be thinking, "How about they just grow up and get over it!" I can understand that sentiment to a point. We should all be professionals and do what we need to do to get the job done. Having said that, all those people were job candidates at some point. What part of that job posting made them think, "Wow, this seems like a great fit for me!!" I can guarantee you that a High I doesn't want any part of a job description that says "Prepare daily reports." (I think I just threw up a little typing that.)

So why did they apply? What drew them to the offer? Is what they are currently doing in the position what was laid out in the job ad? If it's not, is that the new hire's fault or the bad posting? Now I'm not insinuating that we're all writing bad job ads. What I am saying is that we should be looking closely at the advertisements we publish to make sure the job descriptions are crystal clear in their expectations, *and* they match what that person will actually be doing.

Once the job description perfectly matches the job posting, then we can put to use an incredibly valuable tool that links the job to the ideal personality type – a job benchmark.

JOB BENCHMARKING (MATCHING)

When HR personnel interview candidates for positions in their companies, most companies follow the same basic format.

1. Look over the résumé for practical experience, education, skill sets.

2. Have the candidate take some type of skills assessment. In our medical billing company we have a 40-page assessment that measures coding and billing knowledge.

3. Based on those two pieces, conduct an interview of the candidates that pass the assessment and have a good résumé. The typical interview questions are asked.

    a. Tell me about yourself.

    b. What's your greatest strength/weakness?

    c. Tell me about a time when you failed. What happened and what did you learn from it?

4. Those candidates who are pleasant, maybe even funny, and can talk the talk get either a second interview with other staff members or are moved along in the queue.

So let's look at that process from an objective/subjective standpoint.

1. **Résumé**. Objective. We see basics. Having said that, people have been known to embellish. I know. I know. I'm a High S so I'm trusting that everything is 100% accurate.

2. **Assessment.** Objective. Pass or fail.

3. **Interview.** Subjective as it gets. Was the person polished? Were they sick at the time? Were they having a bad day? Were they a smooth talker who could sell sand to camels?

Which of the steps above triggers the most feeling? The interview of course.

That's when we are one on one with the person. We're looking at voice inflection, body language, what people say or hesitate in saying. Some people are just better at being outgoing and positive in the interview environment than others. We can't let the interview be the biggest piece of the puzzle. We need as much objective data as we can get. We need job matching (benchmarking).

Job matching is the combination of the job description that you create and determining the optimal personality style suited for that position. It's that simple.

The job description creator uses a specific tool called "Hiring Insights for Job Matching."[9] When you use this tool it helps you create a template for the "ideal candidate" based on their DISC profile.

You walk through the questions, and in less than an hour you have an additional objective tool to be used in the hiring process. The program will plot out the ideal point on the graph that fits the ideal personality style for the position you just created. You can also use the tool to help move people into other areas on the team after they have been hired to maximize their emotional intelligence and increase retention rates. Take a look at the chart in Figure 12.

Figure 12: DISC and the Hiring Tool = The Ideal Candidate

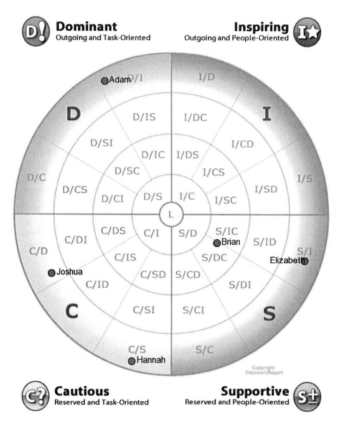

Looking at the graph, who would you say is the best candidate for a sales position? (Tick tock)

I've asked this question to hundreds of CEOs and VPs over the years. I always get several different responses.

Someone shouts out, "Elizabeth!"

"Why?" I ask.

"She should be good with people and can help build relationships with new prospects."

"True. Possibly." I say. "Anyone else?" I ask.

"Brian for sure!" someone says.

"And why is that?"

"Brian's near the center of the circle. He can adapt better than anyone else on the circle."

"He certainly could be more adaptable. Are there any questions that we should be asking ourselves when we're trying to determine the best sales candidate?"

"What are we selling?" someone says.

"Yes!" I respond.

"To whom are we selling?"

Again, I jump back in with "Right, again!"

"What's the sales cycle?"

"Another great question," I add.

"Hunter or farmer?" Another great question.

If we're not taking into account those questions and others along with creating a job matching benchmark, we might hire someone in a quadrant that is completely opposite of where their natural gifts and talents are.

Let's say we use a hiring assessment tool and have the five candidates take an assessment. The hiring tool would plot itself on the graph based upon the responses that are given to it by the hiring manager who created it. I will mark the ideal candidate based on the hiring tool with a star on the next graph (see Figure 13).

Figure 13: Using the Hiring Tool to Plot the Ideal Candidate

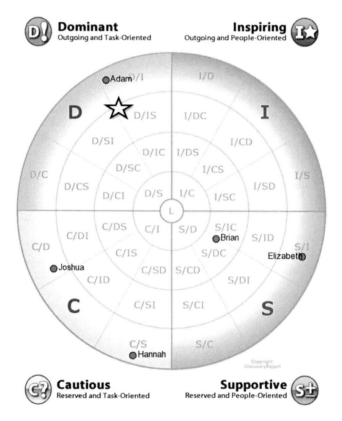

Now, it's very clear to see which person is closest to the star. It's Adam. Based upon the answers to the hiring benchmarking tool, we have identified the ideal emotional profile for a successful person in this role.

So if we were to hire Elizabeth, could she perform in that role as a High D? Absolutely. She would have to adapt tremendously in that role. Every day she would be pushed out of her comfort zone into activities and processes that *drain* her energy. Adam would be *gaining* energy every day in that role because he is functioning in a quadrant where he already feels comfortable.

Elizabeth will not be at this company or in this role very long if she has to adapt this much on a daily basis.

RA TIP: Gone are the days of hiring someone based on their qualifications and experience alone. Today the right fit with the company – the people, the corporate view point, and where the company is headed – is a factor that is just as important.

It's imperative to get your people in the right roles so that they come to work feeling like the job was tailor made for them. If you use a hiring assessment tool, you can achieve that result. Let's look at some more graphs to make other generalizations that may or may not be true based upon what we "think" a role should be.

Let's say that all of these people applied for a customer service position (see Figure 14). If all of them had above-average interviews with similar résumés and skill sets, which person is the *least* likely to stay in that position long term?

Figure 14: Hiring for Customer Service Position

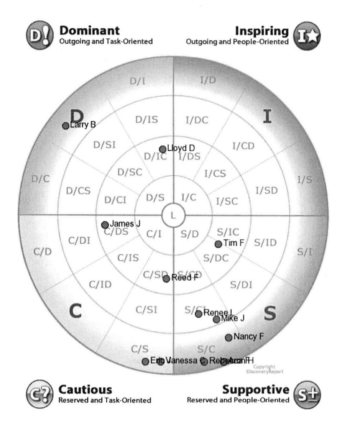

Larry, correct! Larry is in the D quadrant where there is little time for empathy and listening to others. Each customer service position is different. So Larry couldn't necessarily be immediately eliminated from the running for the customer service position. We haven't benchmarked the role yet. Let's look at another example.

Again, all other things being equal, who is the best fit for a position responsible for keeping team morale high? (See Figure 15.)

Figure 15: Hiring for Team Morale Position

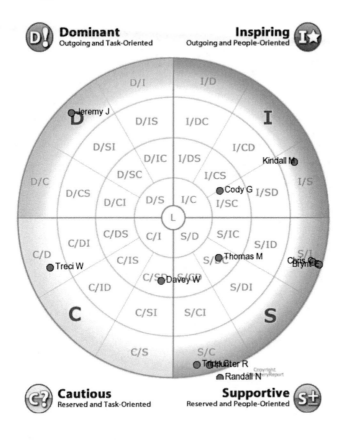

You would think it would be Kindall. She's our High I and a natural cheerleader. Who would be the worst fit for that same position? Treci, the C/D. She's doubly task oriented and has too many other things to do to worry about how everyone else is feeling. Again, if we're not using a tool, then we're just guessing.

Using this tool shouldn't be the only objective measure you use when hiring or moving people to other departments. However, it can cut through the first impressions of an interview and give you a very accurate measurement of a potential employee's job satisfaction and longevity with your company.

DISCovery

Before we wrap up I want to share some final thoughts with you. First off, I want to share some of my favorite conversation starters by personality style.

- *Ds:* Ask them how they got to where they are today?

- *Is:* Ask them about the last place they visited.

- *Ss:* Ask them about their people. How did they recruit (join) such a fantastic team?

- *Cs:* What company metrics are they most proud of?

Early on in the book, I modeled how to connect with each style to get buy in. If you're still reading, those strategies worked. Here are some phrases/thoughts that should have resonated with each style.

- *D: We're not here to sing "Kumbaya!"* I wanted the Ds to know that we were going to have applications that they could use immediately.

- *I: My Sloan/Slaw story.* There *had* to be some smiles on faces when you were envisioning me going DUUUUUUUUUUUUUUUUUUUDDDDDEEEEE in slow motion!

- *S: Showing concern for the importance of relationships throughout,* which are what Ss are all about.

- *C:* Giving you *a* list *of goals and objectives* for why this book was worth your time to read.

Use these same techniques based on your audience and you too will build subtle connections that go far beyond a handshake and "how are you?"

People are personality puzzles. The key to understanding them is:

1. *Understanding Yourself (Your Piece of the Puzzle).* If you don't know your specific style blend, you can head over to The Rapport Advantage Store and grab a basic assessment for less than $15.00 in English, Spanish, and French (www.personalityservice.com/portal/GPPM/store).

2. *Understanding Others (The Other Pieces in the Puzzle Box).* There are adult assessments, ones designed specifically for children, and one for teens as well. Have your family take them. The children's reports even have a section specifically for teachers that gives them strategies for how to best motivate your child for success!

3. *Adapting to Others Around You to Build Better Relationships (The Box Top that Gives You a Big Picture View).*

We started this book discussing Lemonheads. I would argue that people are very much like Lemonheads. They have the initial shiny outside that they present when making a first impression. Then later, once you get past that, there is a second layer, their true self. When we use DISC to discover more about others we can get to the real person underneath. That's the person we want to connect with. That's the person making a decision to:

- Buy your product or service

- Join your company

- Ask to take your daughter out on a date

The more quickly and more deeply we get to know these people, the faster we can build positive relationships. Remember, "You're at a disadvantage without The Rapport Advantage." Use the Rapport Advantage tools to make your personal and professional life more rewarding. I'm here to help you on the way. All you have to do is ask. Best of luck and enjoy the journey of DISCovering more about yourself and others!

ENDNOTES

People Are Strange Creatures

1 www.livescience.com/18392-reading-jumbled-words.html

2 www.youtube.com/watch?v=MLhesmKn4Cs

3 My representation of the Brian Tracy's article "Building Trust and Credibility: 7 Steps to Successful Selling" at www.briantracy.com/blog/sales-success/7-steps-to-successful-selling-by-building-trust-and-credibility-effective-listening-ask-questions/

My Proposal

4 C. G. Jung, and H.G. Baynes, *Psychological Types* (London: Kegan Paul Trench Trubner, 1921). Also titled *The Psychology of Individuation*.

5 William Moulton Marston, *Emotions of Normal People* (London: K. Paul, Trench, Trubner & Co. Ltd., 1928).

6 Walter V. Clarke, "The Construction of an Industrial Selection Personality Test," *The Journal of Psychology* (1956) 41:2, pp. 379-394.

GOAL #1: Build the Puzzle's Outline

7 Jim Collins, *Good to Great: Why Some Companies Make the Leap ... and Others Don't* (New York: HarperCollins Publishers Inc., 2001).

GOAL # 2: Fill in the Puzzle's Center

8 We don't call them guns, because they aren't. Markers were originally designed for loggers to mark trees that were to be cut.

BONUS GOAL: Emotional Adaptation and More

9 www.personalityservice.com/portal/GPPM/store